16-19
MATHEMATICS

D0334190

Newton's laws of motion

The School Mathematics Project

CAMBRIDGE
UNIVERSITY PRESS

Main authors   Stan Dolan
                        Judith Galsworthy
                        Andy Hall
                        Mike Hall
                        Janet Jagger
                        Ann Kitchen
                        Melissa Rodd
                        Paul Roder
                        Tom Roper
                        Mike Savage
                        Bernard Taylor
                        Carole Tyler
                        Nigel Webb
                        Julian Williams
                        Phil Wood

Team leader   Ann Kitchen

Project director   Stan Dolan

This unit has been produced in collaboration with the Mechanics in Action Project, based at the Universities of Leeds and Manchester.

The authors would like to give special thanks to Ann White for her help in producing the trial edition and in preparing this book for publication.

The publishers would like to thank the following for supplying photographs:

page 5   – Ann Ronan Picture Library
page 14 – ZEFA Picture Library (UK) Ltd;
page 16 – L. Jeffrey/All-Sport Photographic Ltd;
           ZEFA Picture Library (UK) Ltd;
           Stephen Dalton/Natural History Photographic Agency;
           Bill Frakes/ZEFA Picture Library (UK) Ltd;
page 17 – K. Kerth/ZEFA Picture Library (UK) Ltd;
page 66 – Quadrant/Flight;
Page 67 – Nicholas Judd;
           ZEFA Picture Library (UK) Ltd;
           Blume/ZEFA Picture Library (UK) Ltd;
page 83 – T.C. Mettier/ZEFA Picture Library (UK) Ltd.

Published by the Press Syndicate of the University of Cambridge
The Pitt Building, Trumpington Street, Cambridge CB2 1RP
40 West 20th Street, New York, NY 10011–4211, USA
10 Stamford Road, Oakleigh, Victoria 3166, Australia

First published 1991
3rd printing 1994

Produced by Gecko Limited, Bicester, Oxon.

Cover design by Iguana Creative Design

Printed in Great Britain at the University Press, Cambridge

British Library cataloguing in publication data

16–19 mathematics.
  Newton's laws of motion
  1. Mechanics. Mathematics
  I. School Mathematics Project
  531.0151
  ISBN 0 521 38845 7

Contents

Sir Isaac Newton 1642–1727

1 Modelling motion

1.1 Mechanics today

Many simple everyday events have results we do not expect. For each of the situations below, decide what you would expect to observe. Check what happens in practice.

Think of other events involving motion which you have observed. Can your fellow students guess what happened?

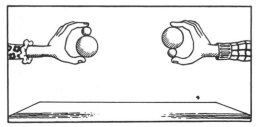

(a) What will happen if a large and a small superball are held, one on top of the other, and dropped together? Does it matter which ball is on top?

(b) A full can of cola and an empty one roll downhill. Which can takes the shorter time to roll down the slope?

(c) A friend holds a bicycle upright. What happens if you push backwards on the lower pedal?

(d) What happens when you stand on a set of bathroom scales and press down with a broom (i) on the scales or (ii) on the floor?

The foundations of modern mechanics were laid by Sir Isaac Newton at the University of Cambridge. He published his **law of universal gravitation** in 1667 and his **three laws of motion** in the *Principia* in 1687.

A study of Newtonian mechanics will give insight into many of the natural phenomena of the world. For example, the tides, the equatorial bulge of the Earth, the time periods of the planets, the paths of comets and the variation in gravity at different latitudes were all explained by Sir Isaac Newton.

Applications of Newtonian mechanics are still extremely important today, especially in engineering, science and technology. For instance, using just A-level mechanics, it is possible to:

- design road humps suitable for enforcing a 30 m.p.h. speed limit;

- estimate the best rotational speed for a tumble drier;

- choose a suitable counterweight for the design of a roadblock for a customs post or car park;

- calculate the height and speed of a geostationary communications satellite.

1.2 Galileo's experiment

Galileo Galilei was an Italian scientist and astronomer whose work at the University of Padua preceded that of Newton. His investigations into the motion of falling and rolling bodies included a study of the motion of spheres down inclined planes. Using planes of about 2 m in length and fixed at angles of between 1.5° and 2°, he discovered a relationship between the distance travelled from rest and the time taken.

Set up and conduct a similar experiment.

What precautions should you take to make your results consistent?
How can you ensure accuracy in the recording of your results?
How can you set out your results clearly?

What is the relationship between distance and time?

Write down your observations. You will need them later in this unit.

1.3 Applied mathematical modelling

When you have progressed with your study of mechanics you will be able to make predictions based upon Newton's laws. You will then be able to use observations and measurements to compare your predictions with reality.

The stages in problem solving are summarised in the following diagram.

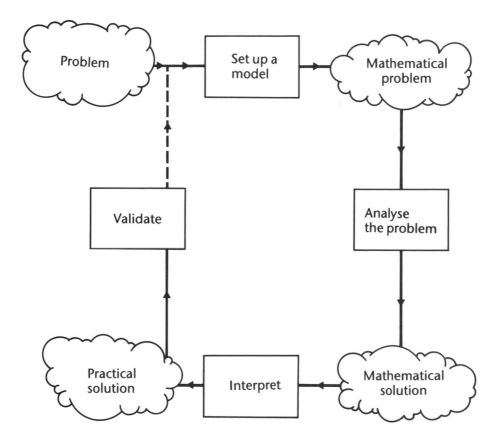

The actions you are expected to carry out during the problem-solving process are:

- identification of interesting **problems** to solve;

- formulation of the problem in mathematical terms, which involves **setting up a model**;

- **analysis of the problem** to obtain a mathematical solution;

- **interpretation** of the solution in real terms, and **validation** of it through your observations or experience.

In Galileo's experiment, the actions you performed can be summarised as:

Problem

This stage requires the identification of a problem to be solved, such as:

- to find the distance the ball will roll down the slope in any given time;

- to find the time the ball will take to roll any given distance.

Other problems include finding the speed of the ball, or its acceleration.

Set up a model

Now you collect data on distance and time. You may choose variables to represent distance and time, d and t. The mathematical problem then is to find a relationship between d and t.

Analyse the problem

You should then analyse your data by drawing a graph and by trying to express d as a function of t, d(t). A function graph plotter or a graphic calculator can be used to find a particular function such as $d = kt$ or $d = kt^2$ which best fits the data and provides a mathematical solution to the problem. Further analysis might give a formula for the speed or acceleration of the ball.

Interpret

You should now interpret your solution in ordinary English language, for example:

the ball will roll 1 metre in 2.85 seconds;
the ball will roll 0.38 m in 1 second;
the ball is gaining speed;
the average speed of the ball in the first second is . . .;   etc.

Validate

These interpretations can now usually be validated in practice! You should check your predictions experimentally and confirm that your mathematical model is valid. If it is **not** valid, you may need to return to the first stage and reconsider your model.

This is an example of mathematical modelling. The function d(t) is a mathematical model of the motion of the rolling ball, and can be used to make quantitative predictions about its real motion. Other examples of modelling will be met throughout this unit in mechanics.

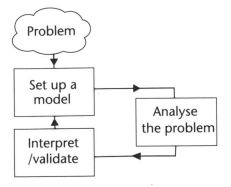

There is an alternative approach, often pursued by engineers and scientists, at the stage of setting up a model. By thinking theoretically about the factors involved in the situation and making simplifying assumptions, they can suggest a formula or equation likely to act as a suitable mathematical model. Observations can be made, the model tested and, all being well, validated.

In 1687, Sir Isaac Newton published a remarkably simple framework for a model of motion which is as relevant today as it was in the seventeenth century. As you work through this unit you will gain an understanding of the three 'laws' of motion which formed the basis of Newton's model.

Three experiments are described on tasksheet 1. You should do **at least one** of these before discussing all the experiments with your teacher and fellow students. At this stage, there is no need to try to explain the results. You should simply attempt an analysis of your measurements to enable you to make predictions which can be tested experimentally.

You will find it helpful to use a modelling diagram for this analysis.

   TASKSHEET 1 — Experiments (page 13)

Each of the experiments will be followed up later in the unit when Newtonian mechanics is introduced. You will then be able to supplement your report of the experiment with some theoretical explanation. **You should therefore save your results for later use**.

After working through this chapter, you should:

1   have some appreciation of what is meant by a mathematical model and how you may arrive at one and test it;

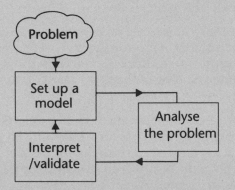

2   understand how mathematical modelling enables you to predict the motion of objects;

3   be aware that there is much you do not understand about the behaviour of things in motion!

Experiments

THE BRICKLAYER'S LAMENT
(based on a story by Gerard Hoffnung)

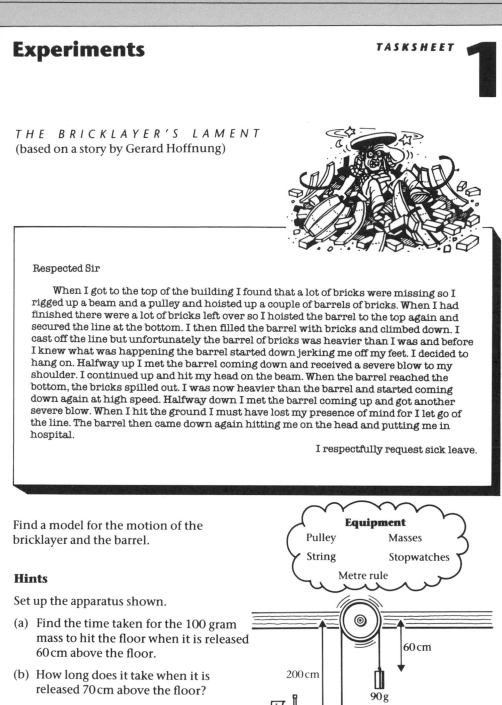

Respected Sir

When I got to the top of the building I found that a lot of bricks were missing so I rigged up a beam and a pulley and hoisted up a couple of barrels of bricks. When I had finished there were a lot of bricks left over so I hoisted the barrel to the top again and secured the line at the bottom. I then filled the barrel with bricks and climbed down. I cast off the line but unfortunately the barrel of bricks was heavier than I was and before I knew what was happening the barrel started down jerking me off my feet. I decided to hang on. Halfway up I met the barrel coming down and received a severe blow to my shoulder. I continued up and hit my head on the beam. When the barrel reached the bottom, the bricks spilled out. I was now heavier than the barrel and started coming down again at high speed. Halfway down I met the barrel coming up and got another severe blow. When I hit the ground I must have lost my presence of mind for I let go of the line. The barrel then came down again hitting me on the head and putting me in hospital.

I respectfully request sick leave.

Find a model for the motion of the bricklayer and the barrel.

Equipment

Pulley · Masses · String · Stopwatches · Metre rule

Hints

Set up the apparatus shown.

(a) Find the time taken for the 100 gram mass to hit the floor when it is released 60 cm above the floor.

(b) How long does it take when it is released 70 cm above the floor?

(c) Repeat for other distances.

(d) Make a table or a graph.

(e) Find a general rule and test it.

(f) Where can you go from here?

SHOOT

Find a model for the motion of a rolling ball.

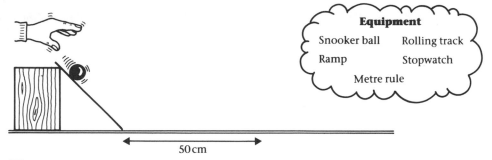

Equipment

Snooker ball   Rolling track

Ramp   Stopwatch

Metre rule

50 cm

Hints

(a) How long will the ball take to roll 50 cm along the track? How long will it take to roll 75 cm?

(b) Estimate how far it will travel in 1 second.

(c) Take careful measurements for several different distances.

(d) Plot a graph of distance against time. Find a general rule for the motion and test it.

(e) What happens if the ball rolls along a carpet or cloth? Repeat your experiment with a strip of ribbon or felt in the track. Remember to record your results carefully.

PINBALL

Find a model for the motion of a ball in a pinball machine.

Equipment

Sugar paper   Water

Wooden blocks

Tape measure

Stopwatch   Ramp

Snooker ball or smooth
hard rubber ball

Hints

(a) Roll the ball gently down the ramp so that it rolls onto the table.

(b) Adjust the height of release so that the ball traces a curve similar to that in the diagram.

(c) Now dampen the ball and release it from the same point on the ramp. Go over the path of the ball with a felt-tip pen.

(d) Using the same release point each time, find how long it takes for the ball to reach A, B, C and D. (A ruler placed as a stop will help you to time accurately.)

(e) Cut round the path and stick it onto squared paper. Mark your times on the graph.

(f) Find and test a general rule.

2 Kinematics

2.1 Motion

Look at things that are moving.

> What questions can you ask about how these, or other, objects are moving?

In this section you will not be trying to find out what causes something to start or stop moving. Rather, you will be investigating what the motion is like.

Traditionally this branch of mathematics is called **kinematics**, the study of movement.

To help describe a real-life example of motion, you can often set up a mathematical model of the actual motion. Various simplifying assumptions are made so that you can study the motion without having to consider all the factors which inevitably complicate matters in the real example.

You might, for example, ignore the size of an object and consider it to be a **particle** – an object whose mass is concentrated at a single point. Furthermore, you might consider the motion to take place in a precise straight line, ignoring any small deviations from such a path. Whenever you set up such a model, you should be clear about the assumptions you are making.

In the remainder of this chapter, you will assume that you can model the motions studied by the motion of a particle. However, you will not need to assume that the paths followed by the objects are straight lines.

The three physical quantities whose mathematical properties you wish to study are all represented on a car's dashboard.

What three physical quantities are measured by the instruments pictured above?

What aspects of a car's motion are **not** represented by these quantities?

2.2 Average speed

One important question which can be asked about any moving object is 'What is its speed?'

In the Système Internationale (SI), the basic units of length and time are metres (m) and seconds (s). The basic unit of speed is therefore metres per second ($m\,s^{-1}$).

On a particular straight road, lamp-posts are spaced every 180 metres. A Scout takes 60 seconds to run between one pair of lamp-posts and 90 seconds to walk between the next pair. He continues along the road alternately running and walking.

When running, the average speed is

$$\frac{180}{60} = 3\,m\,s^{-1}$$

When walking, the average speed is

$$\frac{180}{90} = 2\,m\,s^{-1}$$

Why is the overall average speed not simply $\dfrac{3+2}{2} = 2.5\,m\,s^{-1}$?

$$\text{Average speed} = \frac{\text{Distance covered}}{\text{Time taken}}$$

EXAMPLE 1

Scouts' pace consists of alternately running and walking an equal number of steps; for example, 40 running, 40 walking, 40 running etc. This enables large distances to be covered easily.

Problem

How long would it take a Scout to cover 2 km?
What is the average speed of the Scout?

SOLUTION

Set up a model

Assumptions are made to simplify the problem; if any of these are poor assumptions you can modify them later.

• Assume the Scout's steps are all the same length, 1 metre.

• Assume the Scout runs at a steady rate of $3\,\mathrm{m\,s^{-1}}$ and walks at a steady $2\,\mathrm{m\,s^{-1}}$.

Analyse the problem

The distance travelled in 40 steps is 40 metres, whether the Scout walks or runs.

The time taken to run 40 steps at $3\,\mathrm{m\,s^{-1}}$ is $\frac{40}{3} = 13.3$ seconds.

The time taken to walk 40 steps at $2\,\mathrm{m\,s^{-1}}$ is $\frac{40}{2} = 20$ seconds.

The (time, distance) graph shows the motion of the Scout.

The average speed over 80 m

is $\dfrac{80}{33.3}$ or $2.4\,\mathrm{m\,s^{-1}}$.

The time taken to cover 2 km

or 2000 m is approximately $\dfrac{2000}{2.4}$

or 833.3 seconds.

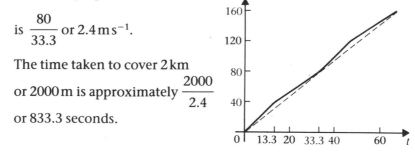

Interpret

Given the assumptions and their likely inaccuracy, a sensible conclusion is that a Scout will take approximately 14 minutes to travel 2 km. The validation of this conclusion will be considered in the next tasksheet.

TASKSHEET 1 OR 1E — *Scouts' pace (pages 32 or 33)*

EXAMPLE 2

A girl runs for 60 m at $3\,\mathrm{m\,s^{-1}}$ and then walks twice as far at a speed of $2\,\mathrm{m\,s^{-1}}$. What is her average speed?

SOLUTION

The time taken to run 60 m is 20 seconds.
The time taken to walk 120 m is 60 seconds.
The total distance travelled is 180 m, and the total time taken is 80 seconds.
So the average speed is $\frac{180}{80}\,\mathrm{m\,s^{-1}} = 2.25\,\mathrm{m\,s^{-1}}$.

EXERCISE 1

1 A jogger runs for 30 seconds at $5\,\mathrm{m\,s^{-1}}$ and then walks an equal distance at $2\,\mathrm{m\,s^{-1}}$. What is her average speed?

2 Find the average speed of a jogger who runs for 30 seconds at $5\,\mathrm{m\,s^{-1}}$ and then walks at $2\,\mathrm{m\,s^{-1}}$ for an equal period of time.

3 My average speed on a car journey of 210 miles (338 km) was 42 miles per hour ($18.8\,\mathrm{m\,s^{-1}}$). If my average speed for the first half of the journey's distance was 30 miles per hour ($13.4\,\mathrm{m\,s^{-1}}$), what was my average speed for the second half of the journey?

4E Repeat question 1 for a jogger who runs at $u\,\mathrm{m\,s^{-1}}$ and walks at $v\,\mathrm{m\,s^{-1}}$.

5E Repeat question 2 for a jogger who runs at $u\,\mathrm{m\,s^{-1}}$ and walks at $v\,\mathrm{m\,s^{-1}}$.

2.3 Graphs of distance against time

In an athletics match, the winner of the 100 metre sprint in the under-13 section took 16.8 seconds and the winner of the 100 metre sprint in the under-18 section took 13.2 seconds. This information could be represented on a graph of distance against time. Such a graph is called a (t, s) graph because the symbols s and t are often used to denote distance and time respectively.

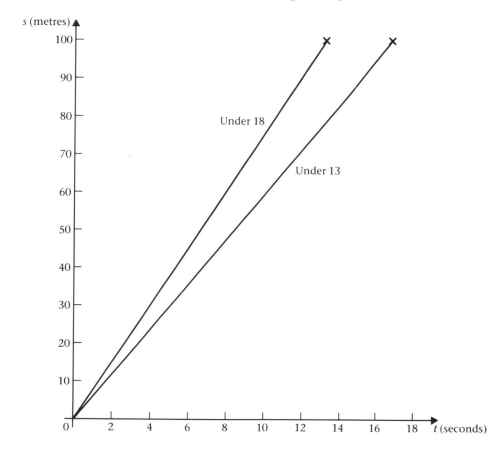

What is represented by the gradient, $\dfrac{ds}{dt}$, of each of the lines above? What information do the corresponding $\left(t, \dfrac{ds}{dt} \right)$ graphs convey about the athletes' motion?

How realistic is this model? How could you improve your model of the motion of the runners?

2.4 **Distance and speed**

In section 2.2 you considered the speed of a Scout alternately running and walking between lamp-posts which were 180 metres apart.

The $\left(t, \dfrac{ds}{dt}\right)$ graph for this is shown below.

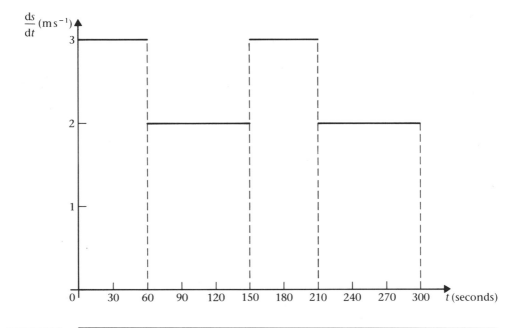

Describe some interesting features of the graph above.

What does the graph tell you about the Scout's motion?

How is the fact that the Scout walks and runs for equal distances represented in the graph?

TASKSHEET 2 — Walking to work (page 34)

For a simple model of motion with speed constant (apart from occasional instantaneous changes), the area underneath the horizontal line sections of the $\left(t, \dfrac{ds}{dt}\right)$ graph represents the distance travelled.

The graph of distance against time for a speed model in which the motion is in sections, each taken at constant speed, consists of jointed straight line segments.

For the Scout discussed at the start of this section, the (t, s) graph is:

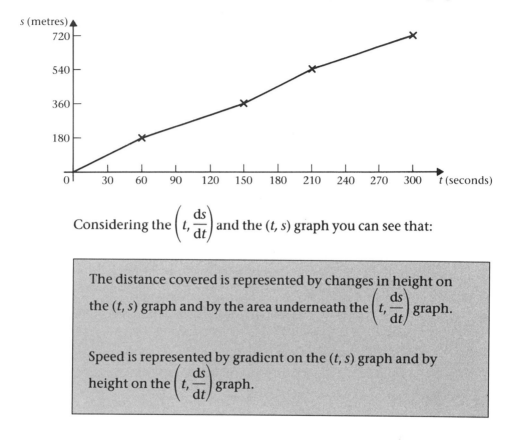

Considering the $\left(t, \dfrac{ds}{dt}\right)$ and the (t, s) graph you can see that:

> The distance covered is represented by changes in height on the (t, s) graph and by the area underneath the $\left(t, \dfrac{ds}{dt}\right)$ graph.
>
> Speed is represented by gradient on the (t, s) graph and by height on the $\left(t, \dfrac{ds}{dt}\right)$ graph.

EXERCISE 2

1 For part of her pre-race warm up, an athlete jogged at $2.5\,\mathrm{m\,s^{-1}}$ for 15 minutes. Represent this on a graph of speed against time. What distance did she cover? On the graph, how would you represent her coming to a standstill?

2 An athlete's training schedule is 20 repetitions of fast running for 1 minute followed by $1\frac{1}{2}$ minutes jog recovery (after each one). If his fast running speed is a steady $4.8\,\mathrm{m\,s^{-1}}$ and his jogging speed is $3\,\mathrm{m\,s^{-1}}$, what distance will he cover in this session?

3 Draw a graph of speed against time for the first 150 seconds of the athlete's motion in question 2. Superimpose the graph of speed against time for someone who moves with the athlete's average speed for the full 150 seconds.

4 (a) This (t, s) graph models the motion of two runners. Draw rough sketches of the corresponding $\left(t, \dfrac{ds}{dt}\right)$

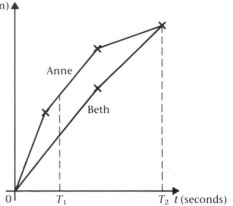

graphs and compare briefly how the runners performed during the race.

(b) What do you notice about the runners at time T_1? Explain how this is represented in each graph.

(c) Repeat (b) for time T_2.

5 A lorry took $1\frac{1}{2}$ hours to reach the motorway travelling at an average speed of $11.4\,\mathrm{m\,s^{-1}}$. It then travelled at an average speed of $16.2\,\mathrm{m\,s^{-1}}$ for 2 hours before leaving the motorway and finishing the journey at an average speed of $10.7\,\mathrm{m\,s^{-1}}$ for 45 minutes. How far did the lorry travel?

6 A team of Scouts challenged a team of Guides to see who could cover the greatest distance at Scouts' pace in 1 hour. The boys decided to run at $3\,\mathrm{m\,s^{-1}}$ for 90 seconds and to walk at $2\,\mathrm{m\,s^{-1}}$ for 135 seconds. The girls decided to run at $3\,\mathrm{m\,s^{-1}}$ for 50 seconds and to walk at $2\,\mathrm{m\,s^{-1}}$ for 75 seconds. Draw their respective graphs of speed against time for the first 6 minutes of the race. Assuming that both teams managed to keep up these paces for the full hour, which team won and by how much?

2.5 Speed

When you say that a car is travelling at 30 miles per hour, does it mean that the car travels 30 miles every hour? If not, what does it mean and how can you measure speed as opposed to average speed?

TASKSHEET 3 — Galileo again (page 35)

The gradient of a curved (t, s) graph still represents speed, but this speed is changing. Speed (as opposed to average speed) is always understood to mean instantaneous speed, so that a speed of, say, $10\,\mathrm{m\,s^{-1}}$ means that the object would travel 10 metres every second if it maintained the speed at that instant.

> On a (t, s) graph, this imaginary motion with constant speed is represented by the tangent to the curve.

You may have obtained graphs similar to those below for the motion studied in tasksheet 3.

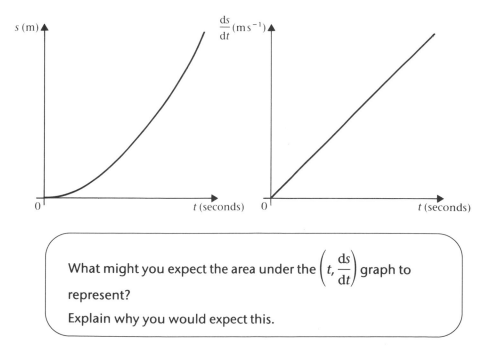

What might you expect the area under the $\left(t, \dfrac{ds}{dt}\right)$ graph to represent?

Explain why you would expect this.

25

Earlier in the chapter you saw that if the speed is constant, then the area under the graph of speed against time gives the distance travelled. Other examples where the $\left(t, \dfrac{ds}{dt}\right)$ graph is a straight line appear to support this theory. It can be proved that this is true for any graph of speed against time.

> The area under a **general** $\left(t, \dfrac{ds}{dt}\right)$ graph represents the distance travelled.

This important and remarkable result is studied further in the *Introductory calculus* unit and is a particular illustration of the **fundamental theorem of calculus.**

E X A M P L E 3

Describe the motion represented in this $\left(t, \dfrac{ds}{dt}\right)$ graph.

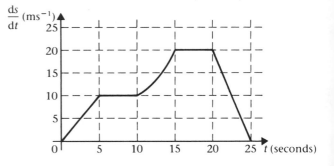

S O L U T I O N

$t = 0$ to 5 There is a steady increase in speed. The distance covered each second therefore increases at a constant rate. The distance covered in the first five seconds is 25 m.

$t = 5$ to 10 Speed remains constant at $10\,\mathrm{m\,s^{-1}}$. The distance covered each second is constant. A further 50 m is travelled.

$t = 10$ to 15 Speed increases throughout. The distance covered each second increases.

> Estimate the distance travelled between $t = 10$ and $t = 15$.
>
> Make similar statements for the intervals $t = 15$ to 20 and $t = 20$ to 25.

EXERCISE 3

1 Tom could not cope with Scouts' pace and generally sprinted, walked or jogged as the mood took him.

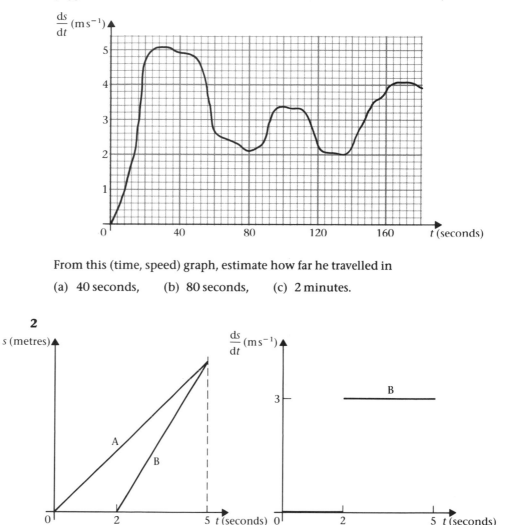

From this (time, speed) graph, estimate how far he travelled in

(a) 40 seconds,   (b) 80 seconds,   (c) 2 minutes.

2

The graphs give some details of the motion of both A and B. At what distance from the start do A and B meet? What is the speed of A?

3 Tracy cycles from Aycliffe to Beford, a distance of 3 miles, in 16 minutes. She rests for 10 minutes before continuing to Ceville, a further distance of 4 miles, which takes 20 minutes.

Simon walks the same journey, does not stop to rest and takes 2 hours.

(a) If Tracy starts out 50 minutes after Simon, where will she overtake him?

(b) What is Tracy's average speed?

(c) What is Simon's average speed?

27

4 (a) Complete the following graphs of distance against time and speed against time for the first 5 seconds of an object's motion.

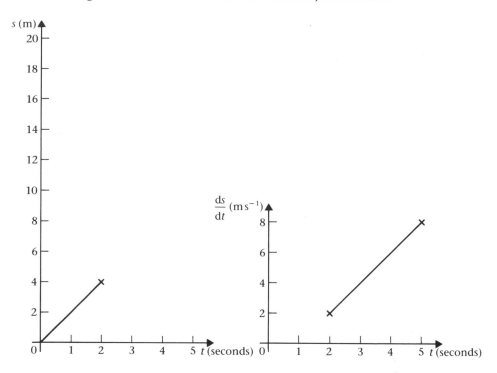

(b) What is the distance covered by the object during this motion?

5

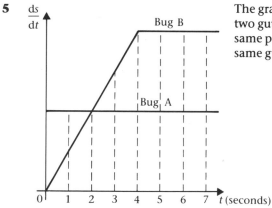

The graphs of speed against time for two gutter-bugs, starting from the same point and crawling along the same gutter, are shown.

(a) Describe the progress of bug A.

(b) Describe the progress of bug B.

(c) When is bug A moving at the same speed as bug B?

(d) When does bug B catch up with bug A?

2.6 Investigating speed

The Highway Code states:

On an open road, in good conditions, a two-second gap between cars should be sufficient.

What is meant by a two-second gap?

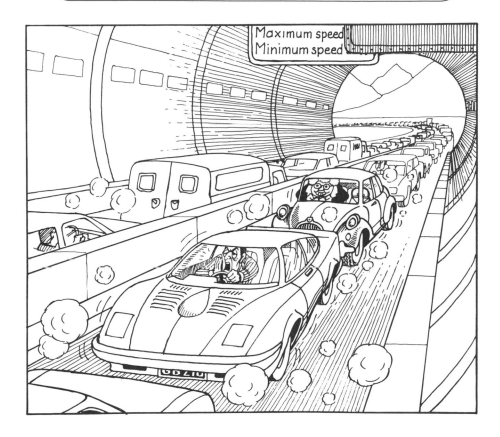

In many tunnels there is both a maximum and a minimum speed limit to ensure a good flow of cars through the tunnel.

Problem

The tunnel authorities want to get as many cars through the tunnel as they can in an hour. The safe gap between cars depends on their speed. Suggest sensible speed limits for the tunnel.

Set up a model

Suppose the cars are 4 metres long and their speed is $v\,\mathrm{m\,s^{-1}}$. There must be a two-second gap between each car. Let the number of cars entering the tunnel each minute be N. You need to maximise N.

<table>
<tr><td>Analyse
the problem</td></tr>
</table>

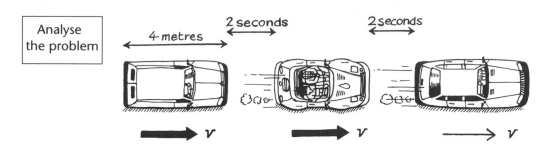

The time between the back of one car and the front of the next car passing a certain point is 2 seconds.

The time taken for one car to pass is $\dfrac{4}{v}$ seconds. So the total time between successive cars entering the tunnel is

$$2 + \frac{4}{v} \text{ seconds} = \frac{2v + 4}{v} \text{ seconds}$$

The number of cars a minute entering the tunnel is

$$N = \frac{60v}{2v + 4}$$

This is easiest to interpret from a graph.

v (m s^{-1})	N
1	10
5	21
10	25
15	26
20	28

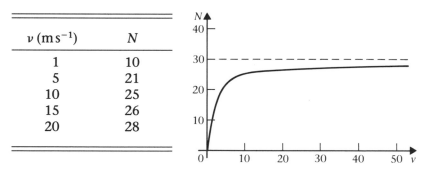

Interpret

You can see that the maximum number of cars a minute seems to be 30 when their speed is infinite. A speed of 30 m s^{-1} will enable 28 cars a minute to enter the tunnel while a speed of 20 m s^{-1} will enable 27 cars a minute to enter. It appears that a speed limit of about 20 m s^{-1} or 72 km h^{-1} will enable a reasonable number of cars to pass safely through the tunnel.

Validate

The actual speed range in the Mont Blanc tunnel is from 50 km h^{-1} to 80 km h^{-1}. In the St Bernard tunnel it is 60 km h^{-1} to 80 km h^{-1}.

TASKSHEET 4 – Overtaking (page 36)

After working through this chapter, you should:

1   be aware that simplifying assumptions are necessary so that motion can be modelled mathematically;

2   be able to discuss how appropriate these assumptions are in simple cases;

3   be familiar with the concepts of distance (s metres), speed $\left(\dfrac{\mathrm{d}s}{\mathrm{d}t}\ \mathrm{m\,s^{-1}}\right)$ and time (t seconds);

4   know that the average speed of an object is the constant speed with which it would have covered the same total distance in the same total time:

$$\text{average speed} = \frac{\text{distance covered}}{\text{time taken}}$$

5   know that speed is the gradient of a (t, s) graph of distance against time;

6   know that the total distance travelled is the area underneath a $\left(t, \dfrac{\mathrm{d}s}{\mathrm{d}t}\right)$ graph of speed against time.

Scouts' pace

In the text a number of assumptions were made about the length of steps taken when running and walking and about the speed of running and walking.

Test these assumptions practically by finding out the length of **your** running and walking step and how fast **you** can run and walk.

1 How near are your measurements to the assumptions made in the text?

2 Set up a new model using your own measurements.

3 Use this model to find your time to cover 2 km when alternately walking and running 40 paces.

4 How does your answer compare with the time of 14 minutes given in the text?

5 Are there any common relationships between variables which appear to hold constant for everyone?

Scouts' pace

Problem

How long will it take to cover 2 km using Scouts' pace?

Set up a model

Different people will have different speeds and lengths of step. Set up a general model to allow for this. Start with just two variables and then add more later if you wish.

For example:
Let the walking speed be $U\,\mathrm{m\,s^{-1}}$ and the running speed be $V\,\mathrm{m\,s^{-1}}$.
Let the length of step for both running and walking be 1 metre.

1   Continue the modelling process.

2   Validate your answers practically.

3   Should you change any of your assumptions?

4   Consider alternative strategies:

   (a) run and walk for equal lengths of time;

   (b) run as fast as you can, collapse and rest, run, etc.;

   (c) run, gradually slowing down, walk, run, etc.

Walking to work

A simplified (time, distance) graph of a college lecturer's (short) walk to work one morning is given below.

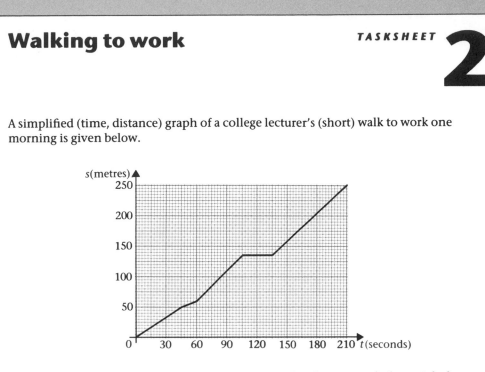

1   Explain the shape of the (t, s) graph by writing a brief account of what might have happened.

2   Draw a $\left(t, \dfrac{ds}{dt}\right)$ graph and check that the information it contains confirms your answer to question 1.

3   How is the total distance of the journey represented on the (t, s) graph and on the $\left(t, \dfrac{ds}{dt}\right)$ graph?

4   What happened 2 minutes after the lecturer left home? How is this represented on each graph?

5   When did the lecturer travel most quickly? How is this represented on each graph?

A S S I G N M E N T

For some particular journey you make (by any method(s) of travel), sketch an estimate of the (t, s) and corresponding $\left(t, \dfrac{ds}{dt}\right)$ graphs. Describe how various features of the journey are represented on each graph.

Galileo again

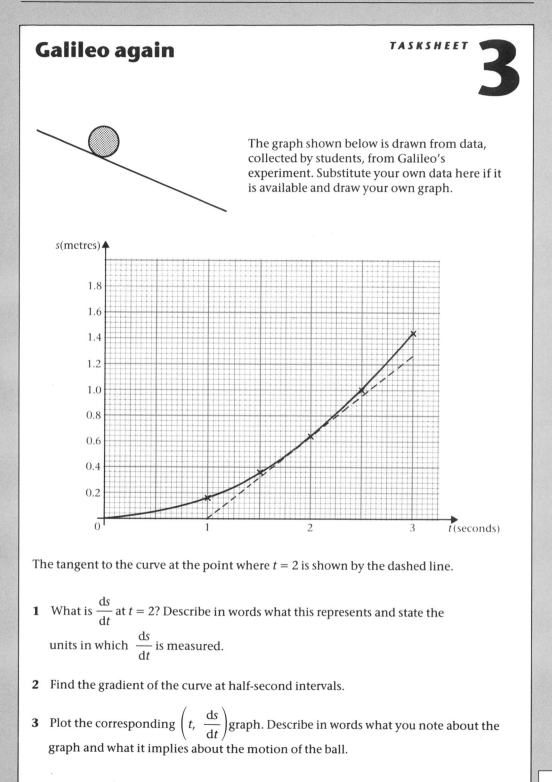

The graph shown below is drawn from data, collected by students, from Galileo's experiment. Substitute your own data here if it is available and draw your own graph.

The tangent to the curve at the point where $t = 2$ is shown by the dashed line.

1 What is $\dfrac{ds}{dt}$ at $t = 2$? Describe in words what this represents and state the

   units in which $\dfrac{ds}{dt}$ is measured.

2 Find the gradient of the curve at half-second intervals.

3 Plot the corresponding $\left(t, \dfrac{ds}{dt} \right)$ graph. Describe in words what you note about the graph and what it implies about the motion of the ball.

Overtaking

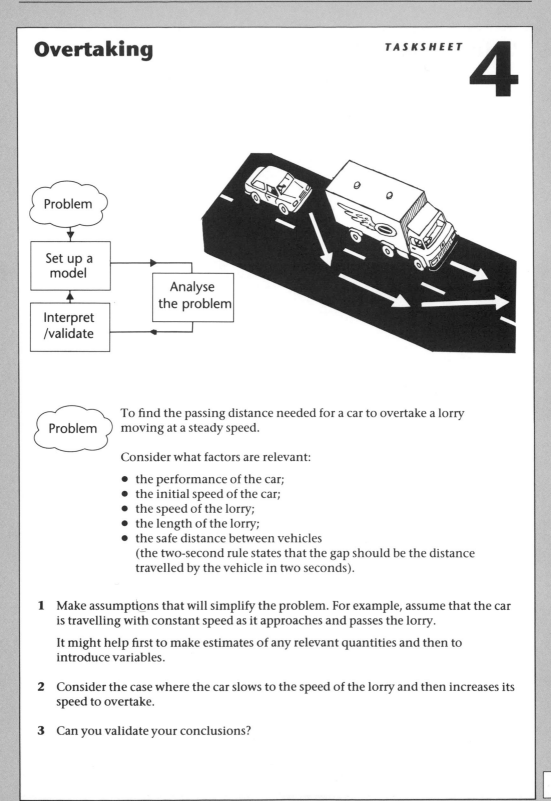

Problem

To find the passing distance needed for a car to overtake a lorry moving at a steady speed.

Consider what factors are relevant:

- the performance of the car;
- the initial speed of the car;
- the speed of the lorry;
- the length of the lorry;
- the safe distance between vehicles
  (the two-second rule states that the gap should be the distance travelled by the vehicle in two seconds).

1 Make assumptions that will simplify the problem. For example, assume that the car is travelling with constant speed as it approaches and passes the lorry.

It might help first to make estimates of any relevant quantities and then to introduce variables.

2 Consider the case where the car slows to the speed of the lorry and then increases its speed to overtake.

3 Can you validate your conclusions?

3 Vectors

3.1 Introduction

A ship has sailed a distance of 10 km and drops anchor. What additional information do you need in order to locate its actual position?

You have just met a case when knowing the length of a journey is not enough. For many purposes it is important to know the **direction** as well as the distance travelled.

When both the direction and the size of a quantity are given, then you are dealing with a **vector** quantity.

Displacement is the word used to describe a distance moved in a certain direction and is an example of a vector.

A quantity which has magnitude or size but not direction is called a **scalar.**

Write down some examples of scalar quantities.

Can you think of any vector quantities other than displacement?

A scalar quantity has magnitude only.

A vector quantity has magnitude and direction.

A displacement involves two pieces of information – the distance between two points and the direction of one point from the other. For example, a ship sails 10 km on a bearing of 037° (compass bearings are angles measured clockwise from north).

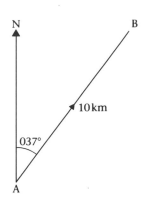

This vector can be represented by the line $\overrightarrow{AB}$ drawn to scale [1 cm : 2 km].

$\overrightarrow{AB}$ is the displacement vector representing the ship's voyage. The arrow over the letters denotes that the direction of the vector is from the first point A to the second point B.

Another way of going from A to B would be to sail 6 km due east to point C and then 8 km due north to B.

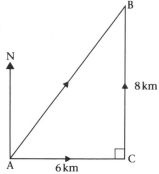

This journey has been drawn to scale [1 cm : 2 km]. If you use a ruler and protractor, you will find that the distance AB is 10 km, as before, and the bearing of B from A is 037°.

Thinking in terms of the rectangular coordinates of a graph, it can be said that going from A to B involves the ship moving 6 km in the x direction and 8 km in the y direction. The 6 and the 8 are called the x and y **components** of the vector.

A convention for writing down a vector in terms of its x and y components is to use the form $\begin{bmatrix} x \\ y \end{bmatrix}$. This is called a **column vector.**

Thus the vector $\overrightarrow{AB}$ can be expressed in two ways:
$$\overrightarrow{AB} = \begin{bmatrix} 6 \\ 8 \end{bmatrix}$$
or $\overrightarrow{AB} = 10$ km bearing 037°

These are two ways of saying the same thing and it is easy to convert from one to the other.

E X A M P L E 1

Sketch the vector $\begin{bmatrix} 6 \\ 8 \end{bmatrix}$ and convert it to the distance and bearing form.

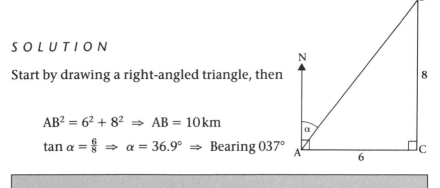

SOLUTION

Start by drawing a right-angled triangle, then

$$AB^2 = 6^2 + 8^2 \implies AB = 10\,\text{km}$$

$$\tan \alpha = \tfrac{6}{8} \implies \alpha = 36.9° \implies \text{Bearing } 037°$$

> The distance from A to B is called the **magnitude** of the vector $\overrightarrow{AB}$ and is written as either $|\overrightarrow{AB}|$ or AB.

EXAMPLE 2

Sketch the displacement vector, 10 km on a bearing 323°, and convert it to a column vector.

SOLUTION

Sketch the vector. Now draw a right-angled triangle.

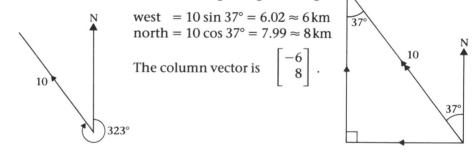

west $= 10 \sin 37° = 6.02 \approx 6\,\text{km}$
north $= 10 \cos 37° = 7.99 \approx 8\,\text{km}$

The column vector is $\begin{bmatrix} -6 \\ 8 \end{bmatrix}$.

EXERCISE 1

1 Sketch the following vectors and convert them into column vectors. Check your answers with scale drawings.

(a) $\overrightarrow{PQ} = 7\,\text{km bearing } 060°$ (b) $\overrightarrow{RS} = 12\,\text{km bearing } 200°$

(c) $\overrightarrow{TU} = 5.2\,\text{km bearing } 310°$

2 Sketch the following vectors and convert them into distance and bearing form. All units are kilometres.

(a) $\overrightarrow{AB} = \begin{bmatrix} 5 \\ 12 \end{bmatrix}$ (b) $\overrightarrow{CD} = \begin{bmatrix} 16 \\ 16 \end{bmatrix}$ (c) $\overrightarrow{EF} = \begin{bmatrix} -5.5 \\ -8.5 \end{bmatrix}$ (d) $\overrightarrow{GH} = \begin{bmatrix} 3 \\ -4 \end{bmatrix}$

3.2 Vectors and maps

Ordance Survey maps cover the whole of the UK. Each map is divided into many squares by grid lines, the distance between two adjacent lines representing one kilometre on the land. Each grid line is numbered, increasing a kilometre at a time. Places are defined by giving the number of the left-hand and lower boundaries of the square that they are in, just as points on a graph are located by x and y coordinates. For example, on the map shown on the next page, the middle of Black Head is at the intersection of the two grid lines numbered 04 and 48. It is possible to estimate a position to 0.1 of a square, or 0.1 km, and so the coordinates of Black Head can be given with greater precision as 04.0 and 48.0.

Similarly, the coordinates of Penare Point are 02.2 and 45.8.

As with graphs, the x coordinate (or 'easting') is given first, followed by the y coordinate (or 'northing').

Whenever a map reference of a place is given, the six figures are written down without the decimal points. Thus:

    Black Head is at 040480,
    Penare Point is at 022458.

It should now be clear that a six-figure map reference contains information about distances, and moreover to an accuracy of 100 metres! Such a map reference can easily be 'dismantled' and turned back into distance coordinates – just cut it in half and insert decimal points! For example,

$$
\begin{array}{ccc}
022 & \{ & 458 \\
\downarrow & & \downarrow \\
2.2 & \{ & 45.8
\end{array}
$$

Confirm your understanding of six-figure map references by:

(a) writing down the references of Phoebe's Point and Cadythew Rock;

(b) stating what can be found at 002480 and at 038483;

(c) changing 024473 and 032505 into distance coordinates.

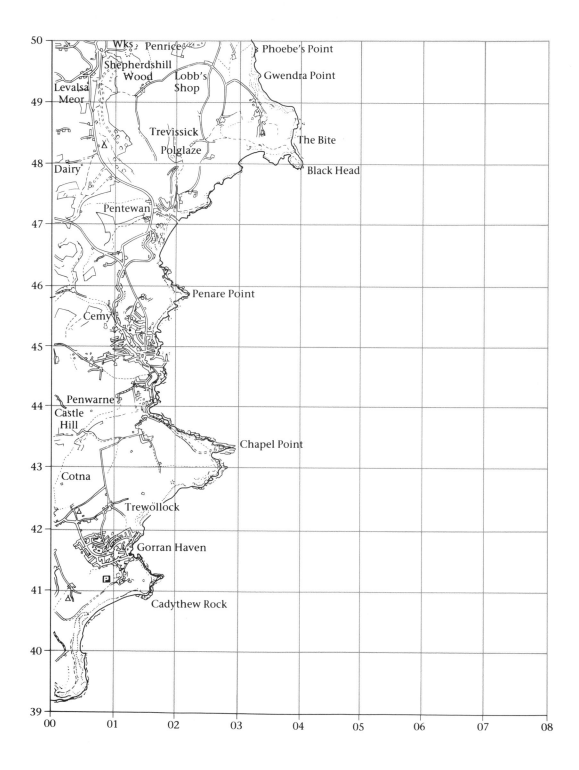

Starting with just the map references of two places it is easy to calculate the shortest distance between them and the direction of one from the other using what you have learnt about vectors.

E X A M P L E   3

Calculate the bearing of Black Head (040480) from Penare Point (022458) and the shortest distance between them.

S O L U T I O N

Start by 'dismantling' the map references, i.e. express them as coordinates.

	x	y
Black Head (B)	4.0	48.0
Penare Point (P)	2.2	45.8
Differences	1.8	2.2

Thus B is 1.8 km east and 2.2 km north of P. Expressed as a column vector, $\overrightarrow{PB} = \begin{bmatrix} 1.8 \\ 2.2 \end{bmatrix}$.

$$|\overrightarrow{PB}| = \sqrt{(1.8^2 + 2.2^2)} = 2.8\,\text{km}$$

$$\tan \alpha = \frac{1.8}{2.2} = 0.818 \Rightarrow \alpha = 39°$$

$$\overrightarrow{PB} = 2.8\,\text{km bearing } 039°$$

This result can be checked by making measurements on the map.

E X E R C I S E   2

Six-figure map references for places A, B, C, D are as follows:

A 015392,   B 227461,   C 100260,   D 312329.

(a) Calculate the distance from C to B.

(b) Find the bearing of D from A.

(c) Find $\overrightarrow{BD}$ as a distance and bearing.

(d) What is the bearing of vector $\overrightarrow{DB}$?

(e) What may be said about $\overrightarrow{AB}$ and $\overrightarrow{CD}$?

3.3 Adding vectors

There are two ways of giving a displacement – as a column vector or as a distance and bearing.

Do you really need two ways of describing the same thing?

Is one form of vector more useful than the other?

T A S K S H E E T   1   –   Adding vectors (page 51)

The **resultant** of a displacement from X to Y followed by a displacement from Y to Z is the displacement from X to Z.

$$\overrightarrow{XY} + \overrightarrow{YZ} = \overrightarrow{XZ}$$

Two vectors can be added by means of a scale drawing if they are drawn 'head to tail'.

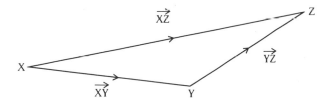

The same resultant displacement is obtained if the two displacement vectors are added in the other order.

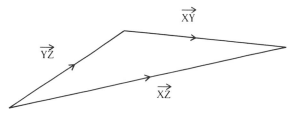

All that matters is that the 'head' of the first displacement vector you draw should be followed by the 'tail' of the next displacement vector.

To add together two vectors in column vector form, add the *x* components together and add the *y* components together.

$$\overrightarrow{XY} + \overrightarrow{YZ} = \overrightarrow{XZ}$$

$$\begin{bmatrix} 2 \\ 3 \end{bmatrix} + \begin{bmatrix} 4 \\ -1 \end{bmatrix} = \begin{bmatrix} 6 \\ 2 \end{bmatrix}$$

The reason they add up in this way becomes clear if the vector diagram is drawn. The vectors form the sides of the triangle XYZ.

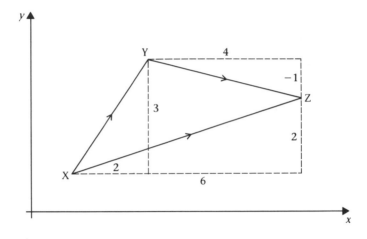

You should note that whereas $\overrightarrow{XY} + \overrightarrow{YZ} = \overrightarrow{XZ}$, it is not true that XY + YZ = XZ.

E X A M P L E   4

Express $\overrightarrow{PQ}$ in terms of the vectors **a** and **b** shown in the diagram.

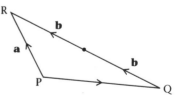

S O L U T I O N

$$\overrightarrow{PQ} + \overrightarrow{QR} = \overrightarrow{PR} \Rightarrow \overrightarrow{PQ} + 2\mathbf{b} = \mathbf{a} \Rightarrow \overrightarrow{PQ} = \mathbf{a} - 2\mathbf{b}$$

E X E R C I S E   3

1 Add the vectors $\begin{bmatrix} 3 \\ -1 \end{bmatrix}$ and $\begin{bmatrix} -2 \\ 4 \end{bmatrix}$. Draw them and their

resultant and show how they form a closed triangle.

2 For each of the following examples, write the vector $\overrightarrow{PQ}$ in terms of **u** and **v**.

(a) 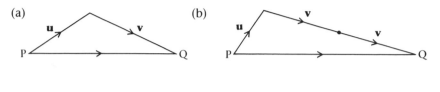   (b)

(c)

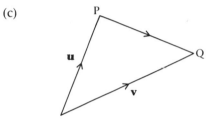

3 Four displacement vectors have a resultant of $\begin{bmatrix} 10 \\ -2 \end{bmatrix}$. If three of them

are $\begin{bmatrix} -2 \\ -3 \end{bmatrix}$, $\begin{bmatrix} 5 \\ -7 \end{bmatrix}$ and $\begin{bmatrix} 16 \\ 4 \end{bmatrix}$, find the missing vector.

4 A helicopter flies from its base at A (025105) to B (105155) and then to
C (195400). While the helicopter is flying from B to C, a second helicopter
flies parallel to it, travelling from A to D where the distances AD and BC are
equal.

(a) Find the map reference for D.

(b) Express $\overrightarrow{AD}$ and $\overrightarrow{BC}$ as column vectors. What do you notice?

(c) What shape is ABCD?

3.4 **Using vectors**

In the discussion point of section 3.3 it was seen that for practical purposes distance and bearing vectors are preferred. However, for adding vectors the column vector form is very convenient and is likely to give an accurate resultant more quickly than a scale drawing.

E X A M P L E 5

One boat of a fishing fleet sails 4 km from a port in a direction 045° to investigate the prospects of good catches. The rest of the fleet travels 10 km from the same port in a direction 120° to its usual fishing ground. In what direction does the single boat have to sail to rejoin the fleet and what distance will it cover?

S O L U T I O N

Let P be the port, S the single boat and F the rest of the fleet.

First the data given is converted to column vectors.

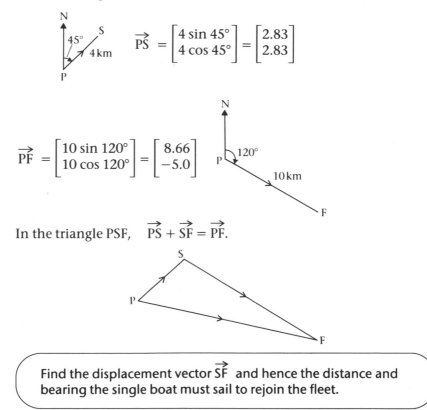

$$\vec{PS} = \begin{bmatrix} 4\sin 45° \\ 4\cos 45° \end{bmatrix} = \begin{bmatrix} 2.83 \\ 2.83 \end{bmatrix}$$

$$\vec{PF} = \begin{bmatrix} 10\sin 120° \\ 10\cos 120° \end{bmatrix} = \begin{bmatrix} 8.66 \\ -5.0 \end{bmatrix}$$

In the triangle PSF, $\vec{PS} + \vec{SF} = \vec{PF}$.

Find the displacement vector $\vec{SF}$ and hence the distance and bearing the single boat must sail to rejoin the fleet.

EXERCISE 4

1 An aircraft A develops an engine fault when it is 83 km due west of an airport P. Another airport Q is 100 km from P on a bearing 315°. Which airport is closer to the aircraft, and by how much?

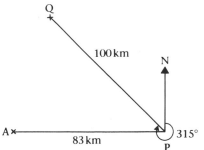

2 A ship S, having sailed 20 km from port P in a direction 127°, dropped anchor and sent an SOS for a seriously ill passenger to be lifted off. At that instant an air–sea rescue helicopter H was 5 km due east of P. In which direction and for what distance did the helicopter have to fly in order to reach the ship?

3 Storm Head Light is 4.7 km east of Black Cap Light. A fishing boat is observed at 2:15 a.m. due north of Storm Head Light. If the boat progresses on a bearing of 322° at 9.0 km h^{-1}, at what time will it be observed due north of Black Cap Light?

4 A hill walker is injured when she is 6 km north-west of Horton. The rescue helicopter is based 20 km due east of Horton. In what direction and for what distance does the helicopter have to fly in order to reach the injured girl?

5 [1 knot is a speed of 1 nautical mile per hour, a nautical mile being 1.15 land miles.]

HMS *Battledore* leaves port at 14:15 and sails at 15 knots on a bearing 119° for 24 minutes, then changes course to bearing 343°, on which the ship remains. At 14:30 HMS *Shuttlecock* leaves the same port and sails on a bearing 205° at 12 knots until 15:00 at which time its engines cease to work.

How far apart are the two ships at 15:00? How long will it take HMS *Battledore* to get to HMS *Shuttlecock* at 20 knots? On what bearing must HMS *Battledore* proceed?

3.5 Position and displacement

At the start of the chapter, the word 'displacement' was defined as describing a distance moved in a certain direction. The word can also be used in the same way as a coordinate or map reference is used (i.e. to define a position).

A fishing boat and a marker buoy are spotted from a lighthouse. If the lighthouse is taken as the origin on an (x, y) grid, then the position of the boat is given by the vector $\begin{bmatrix} -2 \\ 5 \end{bmatrix}$ and that of the buoy is given by the vector $\begin{bmatrix} 4 \\ 3 \end{bmatrix}$.

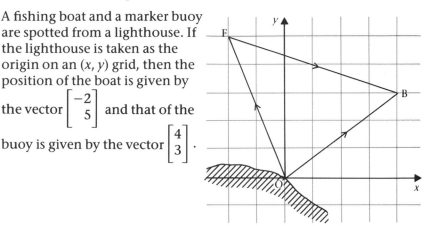

By definition, a **position vector** is a **displacement from the origin**.

Here the movement implied by the use of the word 'displacement' is hypothetical; it can be thought of as the distance and direction of a possible journey from the origin (the lighthouse) even though no actual movement takes place.

The boat is watched (from the lighthouse) as it moves from its position at F to the position of the buoy at B. This motion is defined by the displacement vector $\begin{bmatrix} 6 \\ -2 \end{bmatrix}$.

What is actually observed is a change in the displacement from the origin, and it is this that is used to define the displacement vector.

Displacement = Change in position vector

$$\begin{bmatrix} -2 \\ 5 \end{bmatrix} + \begin{bmatrix} 6 \\ -2 \end{bmatrix} = \begin{bmatrix} 4 \\ 3 \end{bmatrix}$$

Original + Displacement = New
position   position

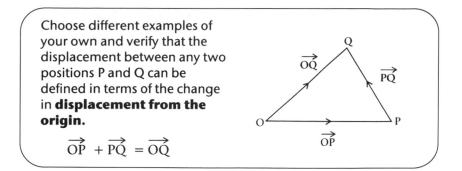

Choose different examples of your own and verify that the displacement between any two positions P and Q can be defined in terms of the change in **displacement from the origin.**

$$\overrightarrow{OP} + \overrightarrow{PQ} = \overrightarrow{OQ}$$

E X A M P L E   6

A plane moves from the point with position vector $\begin{bmatrix} 3 \\ 6 \end{bmatrix}$ km to

the point with position vector $\begin{bmatrix} 7 \\ -3 \end{bmatrix}$ km. Find its displacement.

S O L U T I O N

Original position + Displacement = New position
vector   vector

So $\quad \begin{bmatrix} 3 \\ 6 \end{bmatrix} +$ Displacement $= \begin{bmatrix} 7 \\ -3 \end{bmatrix}$

$\qquad$ Displacement $= \begin{bmatrix} 7 \\ -3 \end{bmatrix} - \begin{bmatrix} 3 \\ 6 \end{bmatrix} = \begin{bmatrix} 4 \\ -9 \end{bmatrix}$ km

E X E R C I S E   5

1   Complete the following table.

	(a)	(b)	(c)	(d)
Original position vector	$\begin{bmatrix} 200 \\ 90 \end{bmatrix}$	$\begin{bmatrix} 7 \\ -7 \end{bmatrix}$	$\begin{bmatrix} -32 \\ 16 \end{bmatrix}$	
New position vector			$\begin{bmatrix} -15 \\ -4 \end{bmatrix}$	$\begin{bmatrix} -10 \\ -8 \end{bmatrix}$
Displacement	$\begin{bmatrix} 126 \\ -9 \end{bmatrix}$	$\begin{bmatrix} 66 \\ -74 \end{bmatrix}$		$\begin{bmatrix} 78 \\ 254 \end{bmatrix}$

2 A boat travels down a winding channel. Its original position vector was $\begin{bmatrix} 5.7 \\ 2.6 \end{bmatrix}$ km and its journey can be described by the successive displacement vectors $\begin{bmatrix} 0.9 \\ 0.2 \end{bmatrix}$, $\begin{bmatrix} 1.4 \\ -0.7 \end{bmatrix}$ and $\begin{bmatrix} 1.2 \\ 0.5 \end{bmatrix}$ km.

(a) Find its new position vector.

(b) What is its total displacement?

(c) How far has the boat travelled?

After working through this chapter you should:

1 be aware that displacement is a vector quantity and has both magnitude and direction;

2 know that the magnitude of $\overrightarrow{AB}$ is the distance from A to B and is written as $|\overrightarrow{AB}|$ or AB;

3 understand that a column vector can describe either a displacement or a position;

4 be able to convert column vectors to distance and bearing form and vice versa;

5 be able to convert six-figure map references to coordinates and vice versa;

6 know that vectors can be added 'head to tail' in either order,

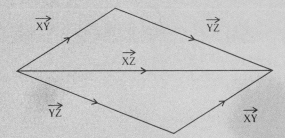

and can be added as column vectors

$$\begin{bmatrix} 3 \\ 2 \end{bmatrix} + \begin{bmatrix} 5 \\ -2 \end{bmatrix} = \begin{bmatrix} 8 \\ 0 \end{bmatrix}$$

7 know that displacement is change in position vector and that

Original position + Displacement = Final position

Adding vectors

1   A police helicopter is monitoring traffic flow. Trouble spots are known to be at X (026102),   Y (134154) and Z (185496).

(a) Write $\overrightarrow{XZ}$, $\overrightarrow{XY}$ and $\overrightarrow{YZ}$ as column vectors.

(b) Can you see any connection between $\overrightarrow{XZ}$, $\overrightarrow{XY}$ and $\overrightarrow{YZ}$? $\overrightarrow{XZ}$ is called the **resultant** of $\overrightarrow{XY}$ and $\overrightarrow{YZ}$.

(c) In what direction, and how far, does the helicopter fly in going from:

    (i) X to Z   (ii) X to Y   (iii) Y to Z?

2   For any vector triangle, as shown, $\overrightarrow{AC}$ is called the resultant of $\overrightarrow{AB}$ and $\overrightarrow{BC}$.

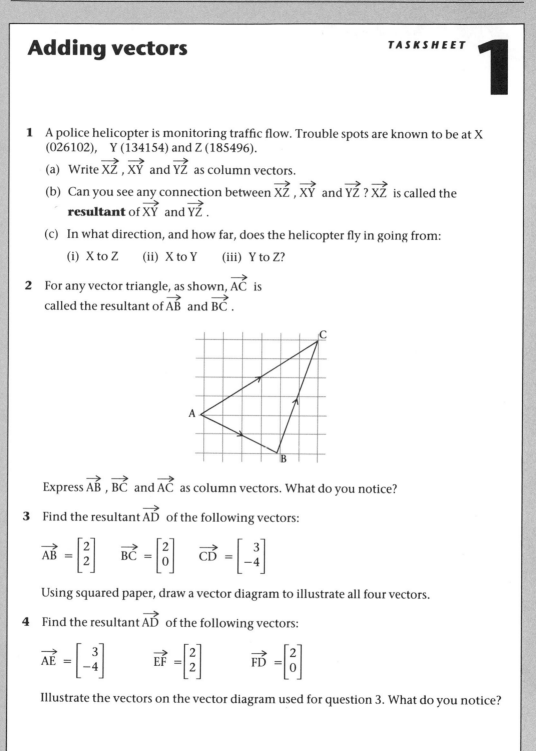

Express $\overrightarrow{AB}$, $\overrightarrow{BC}$ and $\overrightarrow{AC}$ as column vectors. What do you notice?

3   Find the resultant $\overrightarrow{AD}$ of the following vectors:

$$\overrightarrow{AB} = \begin{bmatrix} 2 \\ 2 \end{bmatrix} \qquad \overrightarrow{BC} = \begin{bmatrix} 2 \\ 0 \end{bmatrix} \qquad \overrightarrow{CD} = \begin{bmatrix} 3 \\ -4 \end{bmatrix}$$

Using squared paper, draw a vector diagram to illustrate all four vectors.

4   Find the resultant $\overrightarrow{AD}$ of the following vectors:

$$\overrightarrow{AE} = \begin{bmatrix} 3 \\ -4 \end{bmatrix} \qquad \overrightarrow{EF} = \begin{bmatrix} 2 \\ 2 \end{bmatrix} \qquad \overrightarrow{FD} = \begin{bmatrix} 2 \\ 0 \end{bmatrix}$$

Illustrate the vectors on the vector diagram used for question 3. What do you notice?

4 Velocity

4.1 Speed or velocity?

The speed of an object is simply a measure of how fast it is travelling. In everyday language, 'velocity' is often used in this way as well. However, mathematicians and scientists use the word 'velocity' in the special sense of meaning speed **and** direction.

Consider a car travelling along a winding road.

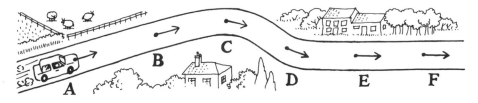

Points A to F show the car's position at 10-second intervals. Over what parts of the journey is

(a) the speed constant,   (b) the velocity constant?

Speed is an example of a scalar quantity; it can, for example, be read from the speedometer of a car without reference to the direction of travel.

Velocity is a vector having the same magnitude as speed but pointing in the direction of motion.

Two cars travelling at 40 kilometres per hour ($40 \, \text{km h}^{-1}$), one going north and the other going east, have the same speed but different velocities. The velocities can be represented by arrows drawn to scale in appropriate directions, or by column vectors.

$$\begin{bmatrix} 0 \\ 40 \end{bmatrix} \text{ or } 40 \, \text{km h}^{-1} \qquad \begin{bmatrix} 40 \\ 0 \end{bmatrix} \text{ or } 40 \, \text{km h}^{-1}$$

4.2 Average speed and average velocity

Just as 'average speed' means the **equivalent constant speed**, so 'average velocity' means the **equivalent constant velocity.**

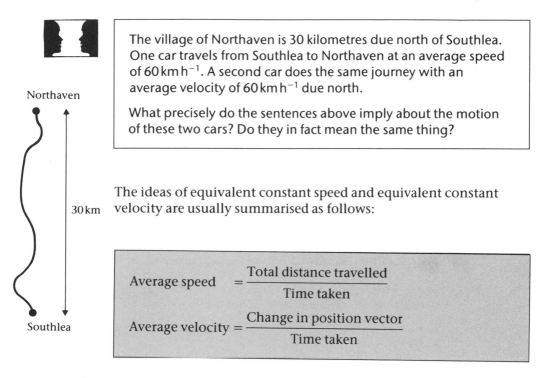

The village of Northaven is 30 kilometres due north of Southlea. One car travels from Southlea to Northaven at an average speed of $60\,\mathrm{km\,h^{-1}}$. A second car does the same journey with an average velocity of $60\,\mathrm{km\,h^{-1}}$ due north.

What precisely do the sentences above imply about the motion of these two cars? Do they in fact mean the same thing?

The ideas of equivalent constant speed and equivalent constant velocity are usually summarised as follows:

$$\text{Average speed} = \frac{\text{Total distance travelled}}{\text{Time taken}}$$

$$\text{Average velocity} = \frac{\text{Change in position vector}}{\text{Time taken}}$$

E X A M P L E   1

Susan walks 2 km in half an hour along a road which runs north and then runs back halfway along her route in 10 minutes.

What are her average speed and her average velocity for the whole journey?

S O L U T I O N

The total time for the whole journey is $40\,\mathrm{min} = \frac{2}{3}$ hour, while the total distance for the whole journey is 3 km.

Average speed $= 3 \div \frac{2}{3}\,\mathrm{km\,h^{-1}} = \frac{9}{2}\,\mathrm{km\,h^{-1}} = 4.5\,\mathrm{km\,h^{-1}}$

Displacement $= 1\,\mathrm{km}$ north

Average velocity $= 1 \div \frac{2}{3}\,\mathrm{km\,h^{-1}}$ north $= 1.5\,\mathrm{km\,h^{-1}}$ north

EXERCISE 1

1 A car travels 20 km at 40 km h^{-1} and then returns along the same route at 80 km h^{-1}. What is the average speed for the total journey?

2 A car travels 30 km at 30 km h^{-1} and then increases its speed to 60 km h^{-1}. How far does it travel on the second stage of its journey if its average speed is 45 km h^{-1}?

3

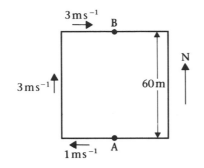

A and B are the mid-points of opposite edges of a square field. Melissa travels from A to B, around the edge of the field, with speeds as shown. What are her average speed and her average velocity?

4 If an object is travelling with a constant speed, then is it necessarily travelling with constant velocity? If it travels with constant velocity, is it necessarily travelling with constant speed? Give reasons and examples.

5 State, with reasons, what can be said about the average speed of a car which travels with an average velocity of 50 km h^{-1} due east.

6

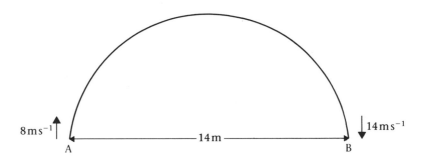

A particle moves on a semicircular path, its speed increasing uniformly with time from 8 m s^{-1} to 14 m s^{-1}.

(a) What is the average speed of the particle and how many seconds does it take to complete this path?

(b) At what point does the particle's speed equal 11 m s^{-1}?

(c) What is its average velocity in travelling from A to B?

7E Because of engine problems, a racing car completes one lap of a race at an average speed of only 40 km h^{-1}. At what speed must it complete a second lap so that its average speed for both laps is

(a) 60 km h^{-1} (b) 80 km h^{-1}?

4.3 Straight line motion

Even for motion in a straight line, there is a distinction between distance and displacement and between speed and velocity.

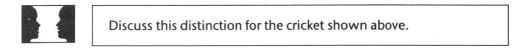

Discuss this distinction for the cricket shown above.

TASKSHEET 1 – Shoot again (page 65)

> The displacement from the origin x and velocity $\dfrac{dx}{dt}$ used in describing straight line motion are vector quantities. One direction of the line is chosen to be positive.
>
> The area under a $\left(t, \dfrac{dx}{dt} \right)$ graph represents displacement. If the area is beneath the axis, the displacement is negative.

EXAMPLE 2

(a) Describe the motion illustrated by the two graphs given below.

(b) Find T and the total distance travelled.

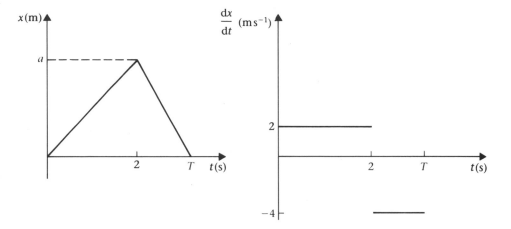

SOLUTION

(a) The object travels away from its starting position with a constant velocity of $2\,\mathrm{m\,s^{-1}}$. When $t = 2$, it changes its velocity to $-4\,\mathrm{m\,s^{-1}}$ and returns to its starting position when $t = T$.

(b) The areas under the $\left(t, \dfrac{dx}{dt}\right)$ graph give the displacement during the interval of time.

The (t, x) graph shows that the position vector increases in magnitude from 0 to a in 2 seconds and returns to 0 after T seconds.

The $\left(t, \dfrac{dx}{dt}\right)$ graph shows that the displacement after the first 2 seconds is 4 metres (the area under the line) so $a = 4$.

It also shows that the displacement from 2 to T seconds is $-4(T - 2)$ or $8 - 4T$, so the total displacement in T seconds is $4 + (8 - 4T) = 12 - 4T$. Hence

$$12 - 4T = 0$$
$$T = 3$$

The total distance travelled is $4 + 4 = 8$ metres.

EXERCISE 2

1 The motion of an object is represented by the graphs shown below.

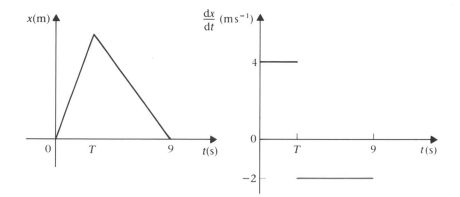

What is:

(a) the value of T;

(b) the distance covered after 9 seconds;

(c) the displacement after 9 seconds?

2 A child throws a ball up from the top of a tower. The displacement x metres from its initial position after time t seconds is given by the formula $x = 6t - 5t^2$.

By using calculus or by plotting a (t, x) graph and using a gradient measurer, find

(a) the velocity of the ball after $\frac{1}{4}$ second and after 4 seconds;

(b) the average velocity of the ball for the first 5 seconds.

3 It is 10 km from A to B. Mary cycles from A to B, starting at 12 noon, at a steady speed of 15 km h^{-1} and then immediately turns and comes back to A at a speed of $7\frac{1}{2}$ km h^{-1}. John sets off on foot from B at noon and walks at a steady speed of 3 km h^{-1} to A.

(a) Draw (t, x) graphs of their motions on the same diagram, where t is the time in hours after 12 noon and x is the distance in km from A.

(b) At what times t_1 and t_2 do Mary and John pass each other and how far are they from A at these times?

(c) At what time between t_1 and t_2 are they the greatest distance apart?

57

4 Part of a (t, y) graph is shown for a ball which is dropped from a height of 10 metres onto the floor.

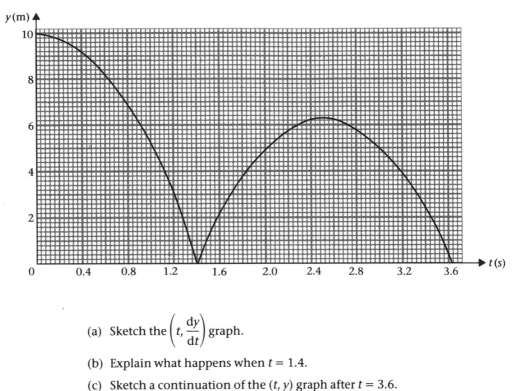

(a) Sketch the $\left(t, \dfrac{dy}{dt}\right)$ graph.

(b) Explain what happens when $t = 1.4$.

(c) Sketch a continuation of the (t, y) graph after $t = 3.6$.

(d) What is the ball's speed when $t = 1$?

4.4 **Change in velocity**

Suppose that three clockwork toys cars are each moving with a constant speed of $30\,\mathrm{cm\,s^{-1}}$ on the surface of a floor mat. The mat is then pulled across the floor at a speed of $40\,\mathrm{cm\,s^{-1}}$.

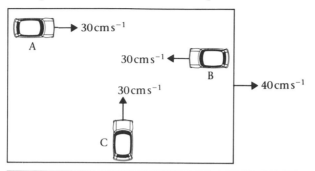

Find the new velocities of the cars.

What is the change in velocity of each car?

What relationship is there between the initial velocity of each car and its final velocity?

When an object moves from point P to point Q, its change in position is simply the vector $\overrightarrow{PQ}$.

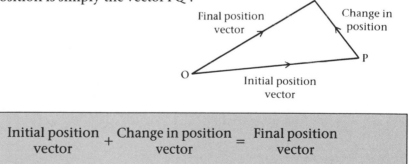

Initial position vector + Change in position vector = Final position vector

The same idea of adding vectors 'head to tail' also works for velocities.

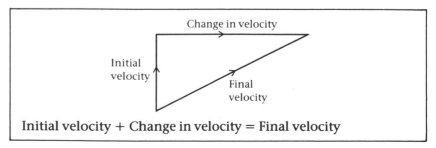

Initial velocity + Change in velocity = Final velocity

EXAMPLE 3

If the initial velocity of a body is $6\,\mathrm{m\,s^{-1}}$ bearing 320° and the final velocity of the body is $10\,\mathrm{m\,s^{-1}}$ due north, what is its change in velocity?

Scale 1 cm: 2 m s⁻¹

SOLUTION BY DRAWING (OR TRIGONOMETRY)

Change in velocity = $6.6\,\mathrm{m\,s^{-1}}$ bearing 036°

SOLUTION BY COMPONENTS

Initial velocity + Change in velocity = Final velocity

Change in velocity = Final velocity − Initial velocity

$$\text{Change in velocity} = \begin{bmatrix} 0 \\ 10 \end{bmatrix} - \begin{bmatrix} -6\sin 40° \\ 6\cos 40° \end{bmatrix} \approx \begin{bmatrix} 3.9 \\ 5.4 \end{bmatrix}$$

EXERCISE 3

1   What is the change in velocity when an object's velocity changes from:

(a) $5\,\mathrm{m\,s^{-1}}$ due east to $8\,\mathrm{m\,s^{-1}}$ due west;

(b) $5\,\mathrm{m\,s^{-1}}$ due west to $8\,\mathrm{m\,s^{-1}}$ due east;

(c) $5\,\mathrm{m\,s^{-1}}$ due east to $8\,\mathrm{m\,s^{-1}}$ due north?

2   A boat is steered north-west at a speed of $4\,\mathrm{km\,h^{-1}}$. It then changes course to travel north-east at a speed of $6\,\mathrm{km\,h^{-1}}$. Find, by drawing, the change in velocity of the boat.

3   An aeroplane has velocity $\begin{bmatrix} 200 \\ 10 \end{bmatrix}\,\mathrm{km\,h^{-1}}$. It changes its velocity by $\begin{bmatrix} -30 \\ 40 \end{bmatrix}\,\mathrm{km\,h^{-1}}$. What is the final velocity of the aeroplane?

4   What is the change in velocity of a particle when its velocity changes from $\begin{bmatrix} 0 \\ -4 \end{bmatrix}\,\mathrm{m\,s^{-1}}$ to $\begin{bmatrix} 6 \\ 2 \end{bmatrix}\,\mathrm{m\,s^{-1}}$?

5   An aeroplane is travelling at $200\,\mathrm{km\,h^{-1}}$ on a bearing 050°. A wind then blows so that the aeroplane ends up travelling at $200\,\mathrm{km\,h^{-1}}$ on a bearing 054°. Find, by drawing, its change in velocity.

4.5 Resultant velocity

As you have seen, the idea of change of velocity is closely connected to that of the resultant velocity of an object in a moving medium, such as a floor mat or a river.

E X A M P L E   4

A boat is steered with velocity $\begin{bmatrix} 0 \\ -3 \end{bmatrix}$ km h^{-1} in a current running at $\begin{bmatrix} -5 \\ 0 \end{bmatrix}$ km h^{-1}. Find the resultant velocity of the boat

(a) as a column vector, (b) in speed and bearing form.

S O L U T I O N

(a)

Resultant velocity of the boat

Velocity of boat through the water $\begin{bmatrix} 0 \\ -3 \end{bmatrix}$

Velocity of water $\begin{bmatrix} -5 \\ 0 \end{bmatrix}$

$$\text{Resultant velocity} = \begin{bmatrix} 0 \\ -3 \end{bmatrix} + \begin{bmatrix} -5 \\ 0 \end{bmatrix} = \begin{bmatrix} -5 \\ -3 \end{bmatrix} \text{km h}^{-1}$$

(b) Speed $= \sqrt{(5^2 + 3^2)} \approx 5.8 \text{ km h}^{-1}$
$\tan \alpha = \frac{5}{3} \Rightarrow \alpha \approx 59°$
The bearing is $180° + 59° = 239°$.

Now consider a similar but more open-ended question.

You want to cross a river in a boat. At what angle should you steer and how long will it take you to cross?

Set up a model

Take a simple case first.

Let the river be 100 m wide and its speed of flow be $1\,m\,s^{-1}$.

Suppose you set off from a point P at an angle α with the bank.

Assume that you can row at $2\,m\,s^{-1}$ and want to land directly opposite at L.

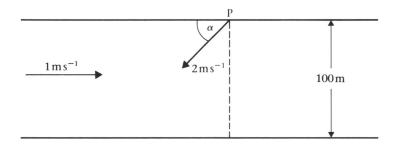

Analyse the problem

You know that your resultant velocity is

Velocity through the water + Velocity of the water

From the vector triangle, $\cos \alpha = \frac{1}{2} \Rightarrow \alpha = 60°$

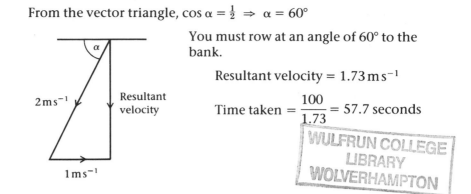

You must row at an angle of 60° to the bank.

Resultant velocity $= 1.73 \, \text{m s}^{-1}$

Time taken $= \dfrac{100}{1.73} = 57.7$ seconds

Interpret /validate

Assuming that you can row at a constant speed for almost a minute, you should reach the other side of the river at a spot opposite your departure point P. If you aim even further upstream you will land upstream.

> Now try to generalise your problem for different velocities of the river.

E X E R C I S E   4

1 A woman walks at $2 \, \text{m s}^{-1}$ across the deck of a boat. The boat is moving at $8 \, \text{m s}^{-1}$. Find the resultant speed of the woman.

2 A girl wishes to paddle her canoe across a river to the nearest point on the opposite bank of a river. If she can paddle at $1.5 \, \text{m s}^{-1}$ in still water and the river is running at $1 \, \text{m s}^{-1}$, in what direction should she point the canoe? If the river is 100 m wide, how long will it take her to cross?

Comment on any assumptions you have made.

3 A river flows with a speed of $1.5 \, \text{km h}^{-1}$. Find in what direction a swimmer, whose speed through the water is $2.5 \, \text{km h}^{-1}$, should start in order to cross at 30° downstream to the bank. Find his resultant speed.

4 A plane with an airspeed of $250 \, \text{km h}^{-1}$ has to fly from a town A to a town B, 100 km due east of A, in a wind blowing from 030° at $50 \, \text{km h}^{-1}$. Find, by drawing, the direction in which the plane must be headed and the time taken.

T A S K S H E E T   2   –   Point of no return (page 66)

After working through this chapter you should:

1 know that speed and distance are scalar quantities;

2 know that velocity and displacement are vector quantities which have both magnitude and direction;

3 be able to find the equivalent constant velocity from

$$\text{Average velocity} = \frac{\text{Change in position vector}}{\text{Time taken}}$$

4 know that

Initial velocity + Change in velocity = Final velocity

and that this relationship can be represented in a vector triangle;

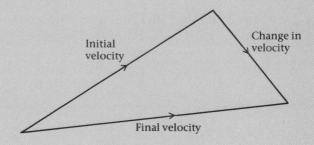

5 be able to find changes in velocity and resultant velocities using either a vector triangle or column vectors as appropriate.

Shoot again

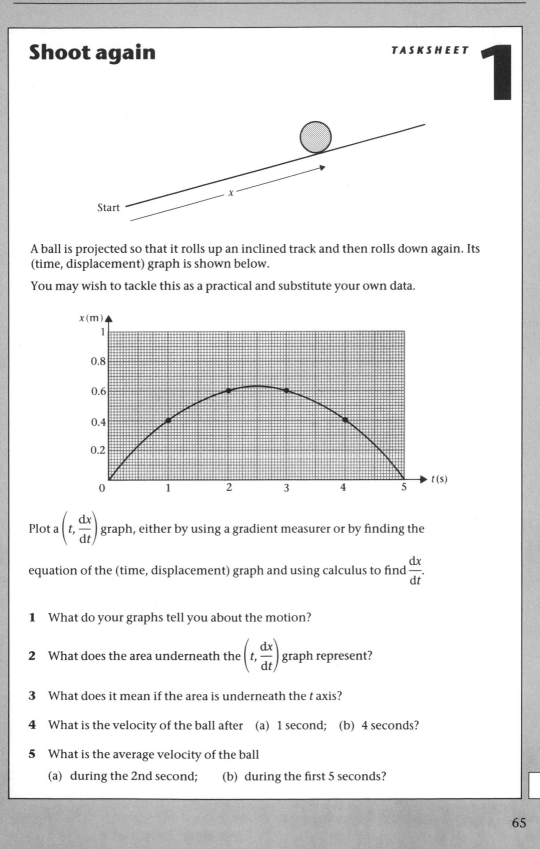

A ball is projected so that it rolls up an inclined track and then rolls down again. Its (time, displacement) graph is shown below.

You may wish to tackle this as a practical and substitute your own data.

Plot a $\left(t, \dfrac{dx}{dt}\right)$ graph, either by using a gradient measurer or by finding the equation of the (time, displacement) graph and using calculus to find $\dfrac{dx}{dt}$.

1   What do your graphs tell you about the motion?

2   What does the area underneath the $\left(t, \dfrac{dx}{dt}\right)$ graph represent?

3   What does it mean if the area is underneath the t axis?

4   What is the velocity of the ball after   (a) 1 second;   (b) 4 seconds?

5   What is the average velocity of the ball

    (a) during the 2nd second;   (b) during the first 5 seconds?

Point of no return

Problem You are the pilot of a light aircraft which is capable of cruising at a steady speed in still air. You have enough fuel on board to last four hours. What is the maximum distance you can fly from your base and still return home safely?

Consider what factors are relevant:

- the velocity of the plane,
- the wind velocity, etc.

Make assumptions that will simplify the problem. For example, you could assume that the wind velocity is in a direction parallel to the velocity of the plane.

It might also help to make estimates of any relevant quantities and solve the problem for these values before you refine and generalise your model.

5 Changes in motion

5.1 The 'quantity of motion'

In this chapter you will study **changes** in motion. So far you have studied the quantities of time, distance, displacement, speed and velocity. These are not the only quantities involved when changes of motion are considered.

What makes a moving object easy or difficult to bring to rest?

Consider different situations in which things at rest are set in motion. What makes it easy or difficult to move them?

Changes of motion of objects appear to be connected with the **mass** of the object. What precisely is meant by mass?

What do you understand by the word 'mass'?

How can you compare the masses of different objects?
Is it helpful to think in terms of the size or volume of the objects?
Can you use the weights of objects to compare their masses?

The mass of an object is the amount of matter it contains. Masses of objects of the same density can therefore be compared by simply measuring their volumes. The unit of mass, the **kilogram**, is now defined as the mass of a certain block of platinum–iridium alloy that is kept at Sèvres in France. It used to be defined as the mass of 1 litre of pure water at the temperature of its greatest density (4 °C). Unfortunately a mistake was made and the kilogram is actually the mass of $1000.028 \, cm^3$ of water!

The pull of the Earth on an object is proportional to its mass and so, to compare the masses of objects of different densities, we can compare the pulls the Earth exerts upon them, i.e. their weights. Greengrocers' spring balances are calibrated in kilograms as if they measured mass but they really measure weight. Six kilograms of apples would still have mass six kilograms on the Moon but such a spring balance would read only approximately 1 kg because of the much smaller gravitational pull of the Moon.

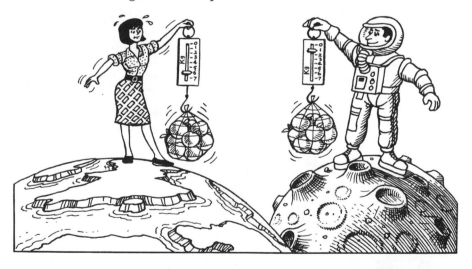

The mass of an object is the amount of matter it contains.
1 kilogram has been defined as the mass of 1 litre of pure water.

In the initial discussion point of this section you saw that the 'stoppability' of an object seems to depend upon both its mass and its speed.

TASKSHEET 1 — The quantity of motion (page 80)

The fundamental 'quantity of motion', as it was called by Sir Isaac Newton, seems to depend upon both mass and velocity. The next section contains some experiments to investigate further the nature of this quantity.

5.2 Collisions

When you consider how wild and apparently disordered collisions can be, it is perhaps surprising that there should be any simple connection between the situations before and after the collision.

A Mini runs into the back of a large lorry which has stopped at traffic lights. What would you expect the motions of the Mini and the lorry to be like just after the collision?

What would you expect if it had been the lorry running into the back of the Mini?

Your ideas on collisions can be checked experimentally.

TASKSHEET 2 — Collisions (page 81)

The effects of collisions on the motions of objects are discussed in more detail in section 5.4.

5.3 Momentum

The fundamental 'quantity of motion' of an object is the product of its mass and velocity. This quantity of motion is called **momentum.**

Momentum = Mass × Velocity

We speak of an object of mass $0.1\,kg$ and moving with a speed of $2\,ms^{-1}$ as having momentum of $0.2\,kg\,ms^{-1}$. This momentum is a vector quantity and you should picture it as a vector of magnitude $0.2\,kg\,ms^{-1}$ in the direction of the object's velocity.

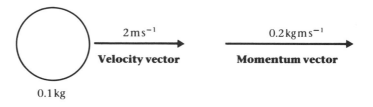

EXERCISE 1

1   Which of the following objects have the **same** momentum?

(a) A 3 kg shot rolled along the ground at $5\,ms^{-1}$ in a northerly direction

(b) A 6 kg shot rolled along the ground at $2.5\,ms^{-1}$ in an easterly direction

(c) A 3 kg shot rolled along the ground at $5\,ms^{-1}$ in an easterly direction

2   A woman of mass 70 kg has a velocity which can be represented by the vector $\begin{bmatrix} 3 \\ 4 \end{bmatrix}\,ms^{-1}$, the components being in the directions east and north respectively. Find her momentum in vector form and calculate its magnitude and direction.

3   Sketch pairs of vectors to represent the momenta of the objects described below, giving reasons for the size of the vectors.

(a) A car of mass one tonne moving north at $90\,km\,h^{-1}$ and a ten tonne lorry travelling east at $30\,km\,h^{-1}$

(b) A speed boat cutting across the bows of a ferry

(c) a jeep racing a rhinoceros

(d) a bullet fired from a rifle and a cricket ball delivered by a fast bowler

5.4 **Conservation of momentum**

In the collisions of section 5.2, you may have discovered that the total momentum after a collision was the same as the total momentum before the collision.

Suppose a puck moving with speed $2\,\text{ms}^{-1}$ collides with a stationary puck as shown below.

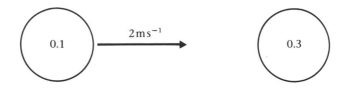

After the collision:

(a) the lighter puck might rebound, for example,

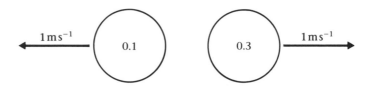

(b) or the pucks might stick together,

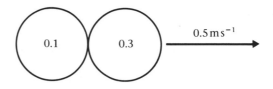

(c) or the blow might be a glancing one.

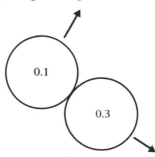

However, in each case, the momenta of the two pucks after the collision will add up vectorially (i.e. 'head-to-tail') to the original momentum of $0.2\,\text{kg}\,\text{m}\,\text{s}^{-1}$.

ORIGINAL MOMENTUM

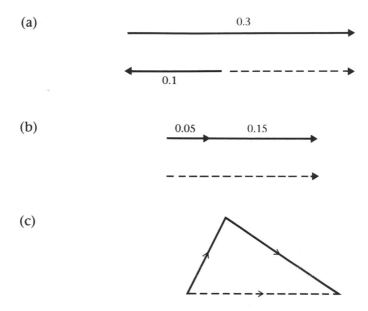

FINAL MOMENTUM

(a)

(b)

(c)

In each case, the final momenta add up to $0.2\,\mathrm{kg\,m\,s^{-1}}$. The total momentum has not been changed by the collision.

When total momentum is unchanged, mathematicians and physicists speak of the **conservation of momentum**.

The law of conservation of momentum is truly remarkable – not only is it simple but it applies to so many different types of interaction. The law applies equally to the motion of subatomic particles as it does to the motion of planets. Rocket propulsion is just one practical application of this important law.

You can use conservation of momentum to help predict velocities after a collision. This idea is illustrated in example 1.

EXAMPLE 1

Louise, on a toboggan (total mass 80 kg) travelling at $4\,\mathrm{m\,s^{-1}}$, collides with Eddie, also on a toboggan (total mass 60 kg) moving in the opposite direction at $5\,\mathrm{m\,s^{-1}}$. The toboggans interlock and move together. What is their speed immediately after the collision?

SOLUTION

In the direction of motion of Louise, the momentum was

$$80 \times 4 - 60 \times 5 = 20\,\mathrm{kg\,m\,s^{-1}}$$

If $v\,\mathrm{m\,s^{-1}}$ is the new speed, then the new momentum is $(80 + 60)v\,\mathrm{kg\,m\,s^{-1}}$. Since momentum is conserved,

$$(80 + 60)v = 20 \;\Rightarrow\; v \approx 0.15$$

They move with a speed of $0.15\,\mathrm{m\,s^{-1}}$.

> What assumptions have been made in answering this question? Are they reasonable?

EXAMPLE 2

Two bodies, of masses 2.5 kg and 5 kg, are moving in a horizontal plane, with respective velocities $3\,\mathrm{m\,s^{-1}}$ south and $4\,\mathrm{m\,s^{-1}}$ west, when they collide and coalesce. Find the subsequent speed of the compound body.

SOLUTION

The total momentum before (and after) the collision can be found by adding the vectors shown:

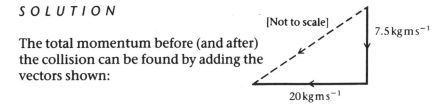

[Not to scale]

$7.5\,\mathrm{kg\,m\,s^{-1}}$

$20\,\mathrm{kg\,m\,s^{-1}}$

The length of the resultant can be found using Pythagoras' theorem. The momentum afterwards is $21.4\,\mathrm{kg\,m\,s^{-1}}$. Since the combined mass is 7.5 kg, the subsequent speed

is $\dfrac{21.4}{7.5} \approx 2.85\,\mathrm{m\,s^{-1}}$.

EXERCISE 2

1 Find the velocity of B after the collision, in each of the situations below.

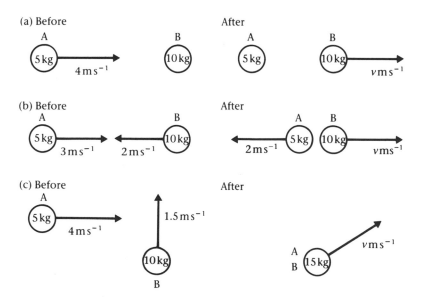

(a) Before · · · After
A · · · B · · · A · · · B
5 kg · · · 4 m s⁻¹ · · · 10 kg · · · 5 kg · · · 10 kg · · · $v\,\mathrm{m\,s^{-1}}$

(b) Before · · · After
A · · · B · · · A · · · B
5 kg · · · 3 m s⁻¹ · · · 2 m s⁻¹ · · · 10 kg · · · 2 m s⁻¹ · · · 5 kg · · · 10 kg · · · $v\,\mathrm{m\,s^{-1}}$

(c) Before · · · After
A
5 kg · · · 4 m s⁻¹
1.5 m s⁻¹
10 kg
B
A
B · · · 15 kg · · · $v\,\mathrm{m\,s^{-1}}$

2 A car hit a parked van and after the collision the two vehicles became locked together and skidded to a stop. From the skid marks it was estimated that just after the impact the common velocity of the two vehicles was $7 \, \text{m s}^{-1}$. If the total mass of the van and its load was 2000 kg and the mass of the car and its passengers was 1200 kg, what was the speed of the car just before impact?

3 A body A, of mass 3 kg, moving with a speed of $4 \, \text{m s}^{-1}$, collides with a stationary body B, of mass 2 kg. After the collision A continues to move in its original direction with a speed of $2 \, \text{m s}^{-1}$. What is the velocity of B after the collision?

4 A body P, of mass 2 kg, moving with a speed of $5 \, \text{m s}^{-1}$, collides with a body Q which is approaching P in the same straight line, travelling in the opposite direction with a speed of $4 \, \text{m s}^{-1}$. After the collision both P and Q reverse their motion in the same straight line with respective speeds of $1 \, \text{m s}^{-1}$ and $2 \, \text{m s}^{-1}$. Find the mass of Q.

5 Two bodies, of masses 3 kg and 4 kg, are each moving in a horizontal plane with a speed of $5 \, \text{m s}^{-1}$, the first in direction 030° and the second in direction 120°. After collision the body of mass 4 kg moves in its original direction but with a reduced speed of $3 \, \text{m s}^{-1}$. Find, by means of a drawing, the velocity of the 3 kg mass after the collision.

5.5 Change in momentum

You have seen that momentum is the fundamental 'quantity of motion'. We therefore measure 'changes in motion' by calculating the **change in momentum**.

Changes in momentum can be sudden, as in the collisions of section 5.2. You can also observe gradual changes in momentum as when an apple falls to the ground.

One of the collisions considered in section 5.2 was as follows:

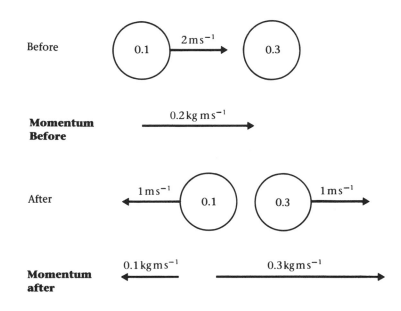

Find the change in momentum for each puck. What do you notice?

Can you explain why this should happen?

TASKSHEET 3 — The effect of blows (page 82)

The change in momentum of an object is a measure of the action exerted upon it. (Newton called the action exerted on a body the '*vis impressa*'.) In the next chapter, you will consider the concept of a force and the action of one particular force, the force of gravity.

EXAMPLE 3

A hockey ball of mass 0.5 kg is hit a glancing blow from a stick so that its velocity changes from $\begin{bmatrix} 6 \\ 8 \end{bmatrix}$ to $\begin{bmatrix} -9 \\ 7 \end{bmatrix}$ m s^{-1}, the axes being taken along and across the pitch. Find its change in momentum in component form.

SOLUTION

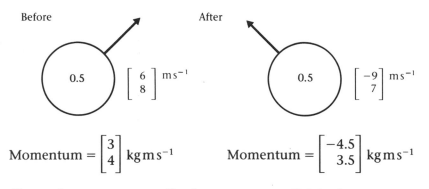

Momentum $= \begin{bmatrix} 3 \\ 4 \end{bmatrix}$ kg m s^{-1} Momentum $= \begin{bmatrix} -4.5 \\ 3.5 \end{bmatrix}$ kg m s^{-1}

Change in momentum = Final momentum − Original momentum

$$= \begin{bmatrix} -4.5 \\ 3.5 \end{bmatrix} - \begin{bmatrix} 3 \\ 4 \end{bmatrix} = \begin{bmatrix} -7.5 \\ -0.5 \end{bmatrix} \text{ kg m s}^{-1}$$

EXERCISE 3

1 A 10 tonne truck is travelling along a straight road. Its speed increases from 65 km h^{-1} to 120 km h^{-1}. What is its change in momentum?

2 A railway truck on a straight track has a speed of 15 m s^{-1}. Its momentum decreases by 15 000 kg m s^{-1}. What is its new speed if the truck has

(a) a mass of 2 tonnes,   (b) a mass of 10 tonnes?

3 A puck of mass 0.1 kg is travelling across an ice rink with velocity $\begin{bmatrix} 25 \\ 2 \end{bmatrix}$ m s^{-1}. It is struck so that its new velocity is $\begin{bmatrix} -15 \\ 5 \end{bmatrix}$ m s^{-1}.

(a) What is its change in momentum?

(b) If the change in momentum was only half this value, what would the new velocity have been?

After working through this chapter you should:

1 know that the 'quantity of motion' of an object is called its momentum and that it is the product of the object's mass and velocity;

2 know and understand that total momentum is conserved if there are no external forces;

3 be able to use the principle of conservation of momentum to help determine motions after collisions;

4 be able to use vector triangles to calculate changes in momentum;

5 know that a blow changes the momentum of an object in the direction of the blow.

The quantity of motion

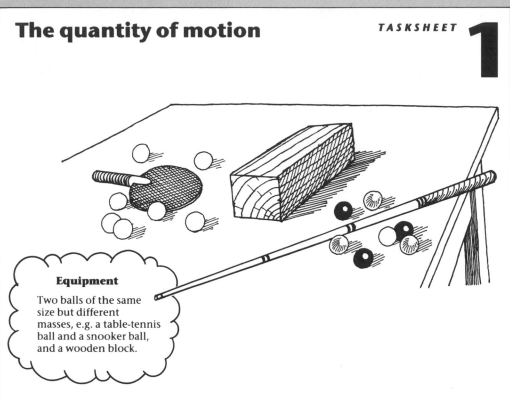

Equipment

Two balls of the same size but different masses, e.g. a table-tennis ball and a snooker ball, and a wooden block.

EXPERIMENT 1

Place a block on the table and roll a snooker ball slowly along the table towards it.

(a) When the ball hits the block, what happens (i) to the ball; (ii) to the block?

(b) Now use the table tennis ball. Try to make it travel at about the same speed. What happens now?

(c) Repeat (a) and (b) using a higher velocity for the balls.

EXPERIMENT 2

(a) Get a friend to drop the snooker ball from a height allowing you to catch it in your hand. Describe what you feel as the height is increased in 50 cm steps from 50 cm to 2 metres.

(b) Repeat the experiment with the table tennis ball.

Is what you feel what Newton called the fundamental 'quantity of motion'?

What do you think are the important factors which make up this quantity?

Which do you think has more 'quantity of motion', a 4 tonne lorry travelling at $1 \, \text{m s}^{-1}$ or an 800 kg car travelling at $5 \, \text{m s}^{-1}$?

Collisions

Equipment

Straight section of track
Two trucks of equal total mass
Assorted masses which can
be placed on either truck.

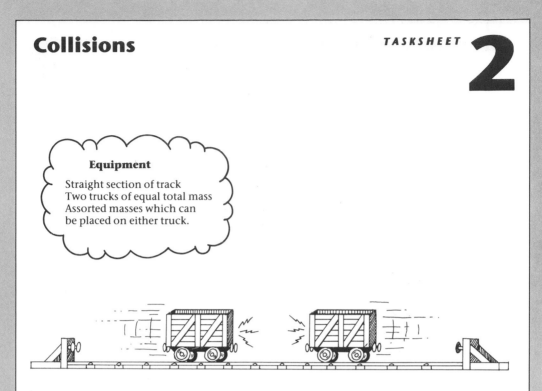

EXPERIMENT 1

Set up the two trucks so that they will bounce apart. What happens if one truck is propelled towards the other stationary truck? Repeat with various masses on each truck and write down your conclusions.

EXPERIMENT 2

Set up the two trucks so that they will stick together on impact. Repeat experiment 1.

EXPERIMENT 3

Try some other possibilities for collisions.

Carefully write down and explain your conclusions about collisions.

The effect of blows

Equipment

Graduated ramp
Balls of various sizes
Perspex ruler (to apply blow)
Table with smooth top

EXPERIMENT 1

Release a ball down a graduated ramp. Once the ball is in motion on a horizontal surface, use the ruler to hit the ball as shown in the diagram. Describe the new motion of the ball and discuss what characteristics of the motion have been altered by the blow. Repeat with blows of various strengths.

EXPERIMENT 2

Repeat experiment 1 with balls of different sizes released from various initial heights on the ramp. Make a careful summary of your observations.

EXPERIMENT 3

Release two balls simultaneously from the same height on the ramp but a few centimetres apart. When both balls are moving on a smooth flat surface, apply a sharp blow at 90° to the direction of motion to one ball, as shown above. Repeat the experiment several times. What happens to the ball which is hit? Explain your result.

EXPERIMENT 4

Devise your own experiments to study the effects of blows on moving objects.

6 Force

6.1 Newton's first law of motion

In chapter 5 you considered the fundamental 'quantity of motion called momentum, and also studied changes in momentum.

To change the momentum of an object you must give it a push or a pull. The important features of a push or pull are its duration and its strength or **force**. For example, a tennis player applies a large force for a short period of time whereas a bowler in a game of cricket applies a smaller force for a longer period of time.

Without pushes or pulls the momentum of an object does not change. This important idea is called **Newton's first law.**

> Unless acted upon by an external force, a particle travels with constant velocity (in a straight line with constant speed).

In 1673, some 14 years before Newton's *Principia*, Huygens expressed this idea as follows:

If gravity did not exist, nor the atmosphere obstruct the motions of bodies, a body would maintain forever a motion once impressed upon it, with uniform velocity in a straight line.

It is important to note that Newton's law states that the natural state of matter is motion with constant **velocity**. An object at rest is, of course, travelling with constant (zero) velocity!

> (a) Once a shot has left a shotputter's hand it does not travel in a straight line with constant speed. Why not?
>
> (b) Suppose your car has run out of petrol and you are pushing it along a level road. If you stop pushing it, it will soon stop moving. Why?

6.2 Newton's second law of motion

In the practical investigation 'Shoot' in chapter 1, when the ball rolls along the horizontal track, the (time, displacement) graph is approximately a straight line.

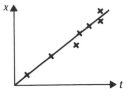

However, when the ball rolls across a carpet the ball slows down quickly and stops.

> (a) Use data from the practical 'Shoot' to find the change of momentum each second when the ball rolls along a strip of felt.
>
> (b) What do you think causes the momentum to change?

There are many forces such as tension, weight, friction, etc, which can act on an object. The **resultant force** is the combined effect of **all** forces acting on the object. Newton realised that if the forces acting on an object are not balanced then the effect of the resultant force is to change the momentum of the object according to the following law, known as **Newton's second law of motion**.

> The resultant force on an object is equal to its rate of change of momentum (its change of momentum each second).
>
> A force which causes a change in momentum of $1 \, \text{kg m s}^{-1}$ per second is said to be a force of 1 newton (1 N).

You may have already met an alternative version of Newton's second law where the resultant force is defined as the mass of the object multiplied by its 'acceleration'. This definition is consistent with the above version of the law and will be considered in section 6.4.

> One form of Newton's second law, for a constant resultant force, is
>
> Change of momentum = Resultant force × Time
>
> Explain how this form is equivalent to the one given above.

Newton's first law arises as a special case of Newton's second law when the resultant force is zero (as for the first (time, displacement) graph for 'Shoot').

In this case, the change of momentum is zero and therefore the momentum of the body remains constant.

$$m\mathbf{v} = \text{constant}$$

Provided the mass of the body is also constant, then the velocity ($\mathbf{v}$) is constant.

EXAMPLE 1

A constant force of 15 N is applied to a body of mass 10 kg for 5 seconds. If it starts from rest, what is its final velocity?

SOLUTION

Change in momentum = Force × Time taken
$$= 5 \times 15 = 75 \, \text{kg m s}^{-1}$$

Since the momentum is initially zero, the final momentum is $75 \, \text{kg m s}^{-1}$ and the final velocity is $7.5 \, \text{m s}^{-1}$ in the direction of the force.

EXERCISE 1

1   A constant force of 20 N is applied for 4 seconds to a body of mass 2 kg, originally at rest. What is its speed after 1, 2, 3 and 4 seconds? What does this indicate about the motion of the body?

2   What force, acting for 5 seconds, would change the velocity of a puck of mass 0.2 kg from $1.5 \, \text{m s}^{-1}$ due south to $2 \, \text{m s}^{-1}$ due north?

3   How long does it take for the speed of a car, of mass 900 kg, to be reduced from $72 \, \text{km h}^{-1}$ to $48 \, \text{km h}^{-1}$ if the net braking force is 1250 N?

4   A train of mass 35 tonnes runs with a speed of $0.3 \, \text{m s}^{-1}$ into the buffers at the end of a platform. What constant force must the buffers exert to bring the train to rest in 2 seconds?

5   A hot air balloon of mass 200 kg rises up from the ground. If the resultant force on the balloon for the first 3 seconds is 150 N vertically upwards, what is its speed at the end of that time?

6.3 Newton's third law of motion

Consider again the collision of two snooker balls. We can model the collision by supposing that two large reaction forces (**R** and **S**) act for a very short time.

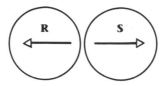

As you found in chapter 5, the total momentum is conserved. By Newton's second law, you know that changes in momentum caused by the forces **R** and **S** are equal in magnitude and opposite in direction. Consequently, **R** and **S** are equal in magnitude and opposite in direction because they act for the same length of time.

This is a particular example of **Newton's third law of motion**.

> When two bodies, A and B, interact, the force that A exerts on B is equal in magnitude and opposite in direction to the force that B exerts on A.

Two students stand on skateboards and press against each others' hands. What can you say about:

(a) the force each exerts,

(b) their subsequent motion?

If one student is twice as heavy as the other, how does this affect your answers to (a) and (b)?

EXAMPLE 2

In deep space, a rocket changes its velocity by firing its engines.
Explain how total momentum is conserved.

SOLUTION

The rocket forces exhaust gases out of its motors in a given direction.
These exert a force on the rocket which is equal in magnitude and
opposite in direction to the force of the rocket on the gas.

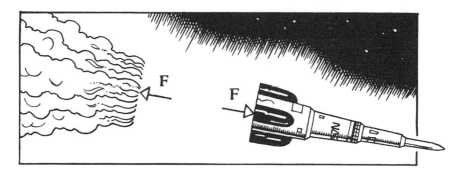

The change in momentum of the gas is therefore equal in magnitude
and opposite in direction to the change in momentum of the rocket
and so the total momentum of the rocket and gas is conserved.

EXERCISE 2

1   For a falling apple of weight W, what is the 'other body' which is involved?
    What is the other force? What can you say about the total momentum of
    the apple and the Earth?

2   Draw a diagram and specify the forces of interaction involved in the motion
    of the Earth travelling round the Sun. Is the total momentum of the Earth
    and Sun constant? What does this tell you about the motion of the Sun?

6.4 Weight and change of momentum

(a) If a golf ball is allowed to fall freely, does the pull of the Earth change as it falls? Sketch the form of (time, velocity) graph you would expect.

(b) If a golf ball and cricket ball are dropped together, which will fall faster? Explain your answer.

Accurate data on falling objects can be obtained easily. Such data are studied on the next tasksheet.

TASKSHEET 1 — The 1 kg shot and the golf ball (page 94)

The force of gravitational attraction on a object is called the **weight** of the object. For an object which remains near the earth's surface, this force is virtually constant. It is conventional to denote the weight of a 1 kg mass by the vector **g** newtons and its magnitude by g newtons. A sufficiently accurate value of g for most purposes is either 9.8 or 10. Correspondingly, **g** is taken to be either

$$\begin{bmatrix} 0 \\ -9.8 \end{bmatrix} \text{ or } \begin{bmatrix} 0 \\ -10 \end{bmatrix}.$$

On a mass of m kg at the Earth's surface, the Earth exerts a downwards force of approximately m**g** newtons.

m**g** newton

For an object moving freely under gravity (with negligible air resistance), the only force acting is its weight and it is easy to apply Newton's second law to its motion. For example, suppose a projectile has mass m kg and that during t seconds its velocity changes from $\mathbf{u}$ m s^{-1} to $\mathbf{v}$ m s^{-1}.

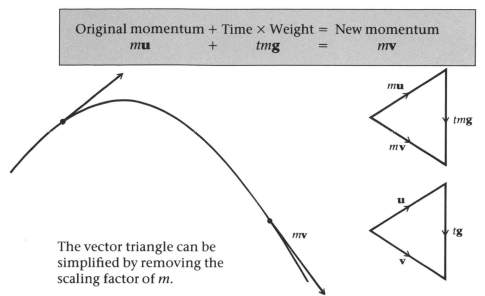

Original momentum + Time × Weight = New momentum
$$m\mathbf{u} \qquad + \qquad tm\mathbf{g} \qquad = \qquad m\mathbf{v}$$

The vector triangle can be simplified by removing the scaling factor of m.

The velocity changes by $\mathbf{g}$ m s^{-1} each second. Another way of stating this is as:

A freely falling object has an acceleration downwards of $\mathbf{g}$ m s^{-2}.

Because of this result, $\mathbf{g}$ m s^{-2} is often called the **acceleration due to gravity**.

The relationship shown in the vector triangle above can therefore be written as

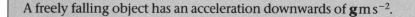

For an object moving freely under gravity:

Initial velocity + Time × Acceleration = Final velocity
$$\mathbf{u} \qquad + \qquad t\mathbf{g} \qquad = \qquad \mathbf{v}$$

A detailed study of acceleration and the corresponding form of Newton's second law

Resultant force = Mass × Acceleration

is given in the optional mechanics unit: *Modelling with force and motion.*

EXAMPLE 3

An apple is thrown vertically upwards at $20\,\mathrm{m\,s^{-1}}$. What is its velocity after 4 seconds?

Draw a graph of velocity against time. When is its velocity zero?

SOLUTION

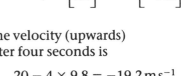

$$\mathbf{v} = \mathbf{u} + t\mathbf{g} = \begin{bmatrix} 0 \\ 20 \end{bmatrix} + 4 \times \begin{bmatrix} 0 \\ -9.8 \end{bmatrix}$$

The velocity (upwards) after four seconds is

$$20 - 4 \times 9.8 = -19.2\,\mathrm{m\,s^{-1}}$$

From the graph you can see that the velocity is zero when $t \approx 2$.

The value from the graph can be confirmed as follows:

After t seconds, the upwards velocity is

$$20 - t \times 9.8$$

This is zero when

$$t = \frac{20}{9.8} = 2.04 \ (3 \text{ s.f.})$$

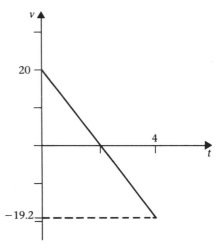

EXAMPLE 4

A stone of mass 2 kg is dropped down a well. It hits the surface of the water 4 seconds later. How deep is the well?

SOLUTION

Set up a model

Assume the stone is a particle (ignore its size).
Assume the only force acting on it is its weight so its change of velocity is a constant $9.8\,\mathrm{m\,s^{-1}}$ each second.
Assume the stone starts from rest.

Analyse the problem

After 1 second its velocity is $9.8\,\mathrm{m\,s^{-1}}$.
After 2 seconds its velocity is $19.6\,\mathrm{m\,s^{-1}}$.
. . .

The (t, v) graph is as shown.

The shaded area under the graph gives the distance travelled as
$$x = \tfrac{1}{2} \times 4 \times 39.2 = 78.4 \text{ metres}$$

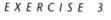

| Interpret /validate |

The stone travels 78.4 metres so the well is at least 78.4 metres deep.

EXERCISE 3

(Take $g = 9.8 \, \text{m s}^{-2}$.)

1 A ball rolls over a high cliff.

(a) What is its velocity after 3 seconds?

(b) How far has it fallen?

(c) It hits the ground after 3.5 seconds. How high was the cliff?

2 A stone is thrown vertically upwards to dislodge a conker on a tree. The maximum speed the stone can be thrown with is $14.8 \, \text{m s}^{-1}$ and it must hit the conker with a speed of at least $5 \, \text{m s}^{-1}$ to dislodge it.

(a) Draw a graph of velocity against time for the motion of the stone.

(b) Use this to calculate the height of the highest conker it can dislodge.

3 A paint tin is dislodged from a workman's platform 70 metres above the street.

(a) Draw a graph of velocity against time for its motion.

(b) Use your graph to calculate the velocity with which it hits the ground.

4 A girl of mass 25 kg and her father of mass 75 kg both jump off the 10 metre board into a swimming pool. What is the momentum of

(a) the girl,   (b) her father,

when they reach the water?

5 A pile driver of mass 2 tonnes has a momentum of $16000 \, \text{kg m s}^{-1}$ when it hits the ground. What height was it dropped from?

6.5 Predicting motion

In working through this unit you have been retracing the work of mathematicians in trying to **explain** changes in motion. Now that you know Newton's laws, you are in a position to **predict** some aspects of motion. It is the essential purpose of all applied mathematics to make theoretical predictions. It is important to know, in advance, how much fuel is needed to land a spaceship on the Moon safely or at what angle to point a cannon so that the human cannon ball will land safely in the net. Trial and error is not always satisfactory!

In your practical experiments in chapter 1 you have so far **described** the motion and analysed the change in momentum involved in each case. Now you know how a change in momentum is caused by a resultant force and you should be in a position to complete the report on your practical investigation in chapter 1, including comments on the forces involved.

In future units you will learn to model many types of motion theoretically using force analysis.

After working through this chapter you should:

1 know Newton's three laws of motion:

- unless acted upon by an external force, a particle travels with constant velocity;

- resultant force equals rate of change of momentum;

- when two bodies interact, they exert equal but opposite forces upon each other;

2 know that a force of magnitude 1 newton gives a mass of 1 kg a change in velocity of $1\,\mathrm{m\,s^{-1}}$ each second;

3 know that, on the Earth's surface, a mass of m kg has a weight of mg newtons, where $g \approx 9.8$;

4 be able to apply the result that, for bodies moving freely under the gravitational attraction of the Earth,

$$\mathbf{v} = \mathbf{u} + t\mathbf{g}$$

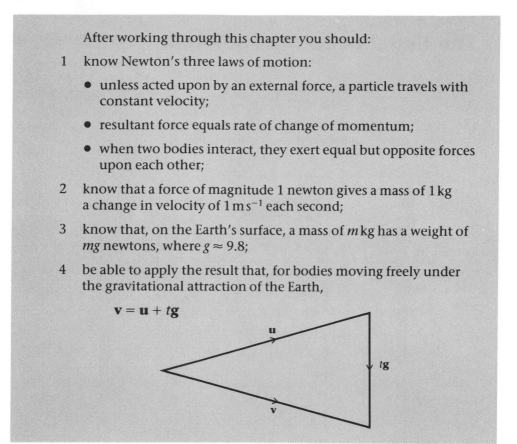

The 1 kg shot and the golf ball

1 A 1 kg shot is dropped vertically from rest. From the photograph of its motion, an accurate (time, displacement) graph has been drawn.

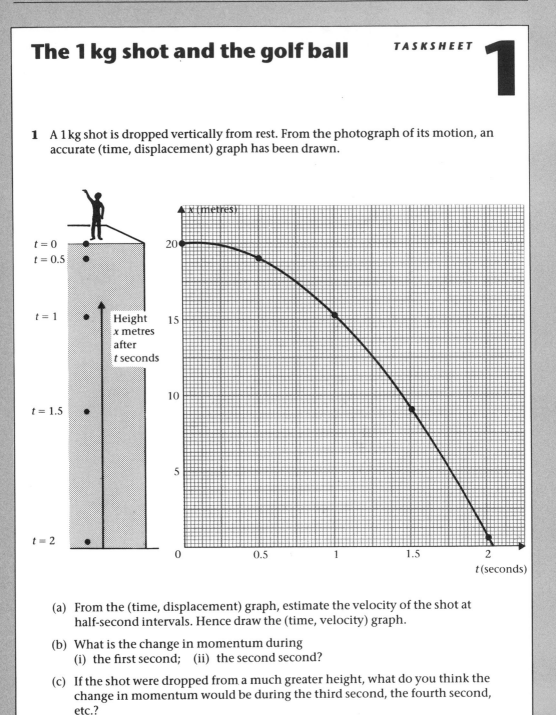

(a) From the (time, displacement) graph, estimate the velocity of the shot at half-second intervals. Hence draw the (time, velocity) graph.

(b) What is the change in momentum during
    (i) the first second;   (ii) the second second?

(c) If the shot were dropped from a much greater height, what do you think the change in momentum would be during the third second, the fourth second, etc.?

(d) What do you think causes this change in momentum?

2 The track of a golf ball as it is pitched onto the green is given below. It has been marked out every quarter second for the first six seconds of its flight.

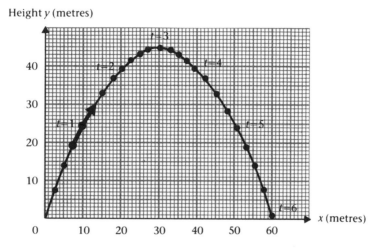

(a) To estimate the velocity of the ball one second after being hit, the displacement vector from $t = 0.75$ to $t = 1.25$ has been marked on the diagram. This is the displacement during a half second. A vector parallel to this but of twice the length therefore represents the average velocity during this time interval. This average velocity will be a good approximation to the velocity after one second.

Repeat this to find the velocity when $t = 2, 3, 4$ and 5 seconds.

(b) The mass of the ball is 0.1 kg. Find the five vectors representing the momenta of the ball 1, 2, 3, 4 and 5 seconds after being hit.

Draw them all with the same initial point:

$t=1$

$t=2$

etc.

(c) What do you notice about these five vectors and what does this imply about the motion of the ball?

Find the changes in momentum of the ball during the second, third, fourth and fifth seconds of its flight.

(d) What do you notice about these changes in momentum? Try to explain what you find.

Solutions

2 Kinematics

2.1 Motion

What questions can you ask about how these, or other, objects are moving?

What direction is it moving in?
How fast is it travelling?
Is its speed changing?
What makes it move?

There are many other questions as well.

What three physical quantities are measured by the instruments pictured above?

What aspects of a car's motion are **not** represented by these quantities?

The quantities measured are time (clock), distance (mileometer) and speed (speedometer). Anything connected with the direction of the car's motion is not represented. The quantities do not refer to the motion of all points of the car. For example, points on the car's steering wheel or on the tyres are not appropriately represented by these quantities.

2.2 Average speed

EXERCISE 1

1 Distance covered in 30 seconds = 30 × 5 metres = 150 metres

Time taken for next 150 metres $= \dfrac{150}{2} = 75$ seconds

Average speed $= \dfrac{150 + 150}{30 + 75} = 2.9\,\mathrm{m\,s^{-1}}$

2   Distance covered in first 30 seconds = 150 metres
Distance covered in second 30 seconds = 60 metres

$$\text{Average speed} = \frac{150 + 60}{30 + 30} = 3.5\,\text{ms}^{-1}$$

3   The total time for the journey was $\dfrac{210}{42} = 5$ hours. The time for the first

half of the journey's distance was $\dfrac{105}{30} = 3.5$ hours and so the average

speed for the second half was $\dfrac{105}{1.5} = 70$ miles per hour ($31.3\,\text{ms}^{-1}$).

4E   Running: $30u$ metres in 30 seconds

Walking: $30u$ metres in $\dfrac{30u}{v}$ seconds

$$\frac{30u + 30u}{30 + \dfrac{30u}{v}} = \frac{2uv}{u + v}\,\text{ms}^{-1}$$

5E $\dfrac{30u + 30v}{60} = \dfrac{u + v}{2}\,\text{ms}^{-1}$

You can use the arithmetic average of the speeds if the jogger runs and walks
for equal lengths of time.

2.4   Distance and speed

EXERCISE 2

1   Distance covered = $15 \times 60 \times 2.5 = 2250\,\text{m}$ (or $2.25\,\text{km}$)

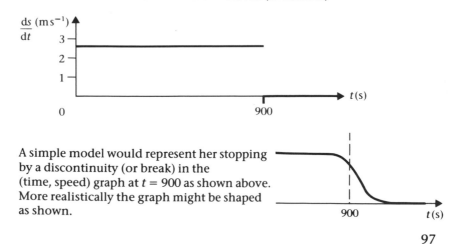

A simple model would represent her stopping
by a discontinuity (or break) in the
(time, speed) graph at $t = 900$ as shown above.
More realistically the graph might be shaped
as shown.

2 Running distance = 4.8×60 = 288 metres
Jogging distance = 3.0×90 = 270 metres

Total distance covered is $20 \times (288 + 270)$ = 11 160 metres

3

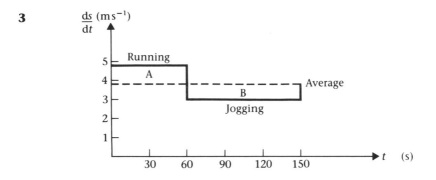

Note that area A and area B are equal. The distance travelled is the same.

4 (a)

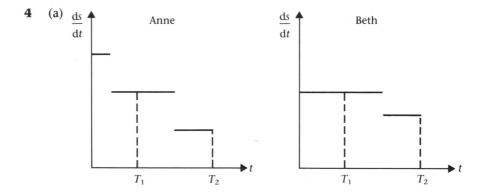

Anne set off quickly but soon slowed down and then finished the race at an even slower pace. Beth maintained a steady pace for most of the race (the same as Anne's middle pace) and then slowed down to a somewhat higher finishing pace than Anne. They finished the race together.

(b) At T_1, they have the same speed. The (t, s) graphs have equal gradients; the $\left(t, \dfrac{ds}{dt}\right)$ graphs have the same heights.

(c) At T_2, they have covered the same distance. The (t, s) graphs have equal heights; the areas under the $\left(t, \dfrac{ds}{dt}\right)$ graphs are equal.

5 Distance to motorway $= 11.4 \times 1.5 \times 3600 = 61\,560\,\text{m}$
Distance on motorway $= 16.2 \times 2 \times 3600 \quad = 116\,640\,\text{m}$
Distance after motorway $= 10.7 \times 45 \times 60 \quad = 28\,890\,\text{m}$

Total distance $= 207.09\,\text{km}$ (say $207\,\text{km}$)

6

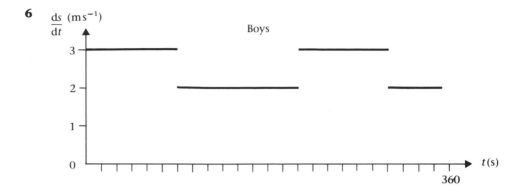

In 1 hour the boys complete 16 repetitions of $(2 \times 270)\,\text{m}$, i.e. $8640\,\text{m}$.

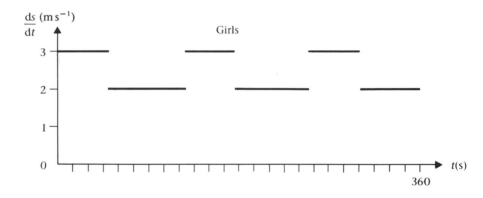

In 52 minutes 20 seconds the girls complete 28 repetitions of $(2 \times 150)\,\text{m}$, i.e. $8400\,\text{m}$. In the remaining 100 seconds the girls complete the $150\,\text{m}$ running phase and walk for 50 seconds at $2\,\text{m s}^{-1}$, covering a further $250\,\text{m}$. The girls therefore win by 10 metres.

2.5 Speed

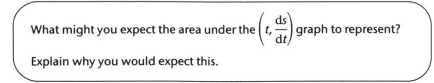

What might you expect the area under the $\left(t, \dfrac{ds}{dt}\right)$ graph to represent?

Explain why you would expect this.

You would expect the area under the $\left(t, \dfrac{ds}{dt}\right)$ graph to represent the total distance travelled. This is because, for any value of T, the area A is equal to the value of s on the equivalent (s, t) graph.

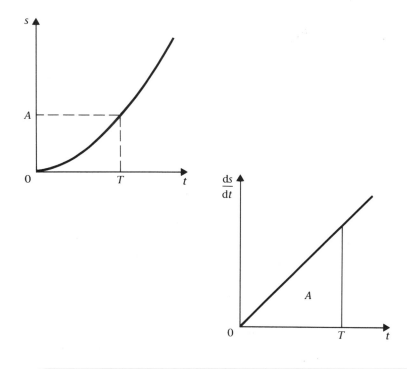

Estimate the distance travelled between $t = 10$ and $t = 15$.

Make similar statements for the intervals $t = 15$ to 20 and $t = 20$ to 25.

The area under the curve between $t = 10$ and $t = 15$ is just less than 75 metres. The speed is increasing, but not at a steady rate.

$t = 15$ to 20   The speed remains constant at $20\,\mathrm{m\,s^{-1}}$. A further 100 metres is covered.

$t = 20$ to 25   The object slows down at a constant rate until it is stationary. The distance covered each second steadily decreases. A total distance of 50 metres is covered in this period.

E X E R C I S E 3

1 Each 1 cm square represents 20 metres and each small square represents

$\dfrac{20}{25} = 0.8$ metres. Estimates to 3 s.f. are:

(a) 132 metres, (b) 267 metres, (c) 381 metres.

2 B starts 2 seconds later than A from the same point and walks in the same direction but at a greater speed. B covers $3 \times 3 = 9$ metres. A and B therefore meet 9 metres from the start.

A's speed is $\dfrac{9}{5} = 1.8\,\mathrm{m\,s^{-1}}$.

3

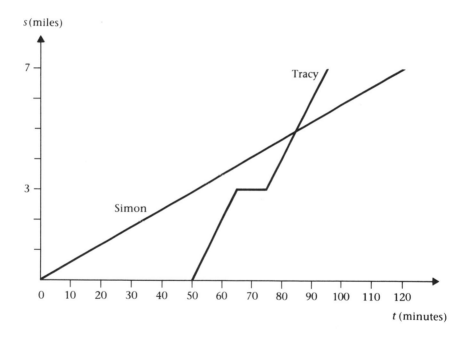

(a) Approximately 2 miles from Ceville

(b) $7 \div 46 = 0.152$ miles per minute, $0.152 \times 60 \approx 9.1$ miles per hour

(c) $7 \div 2 = 3.5$ miles per hour

[It is assumed that, when travelling, Simon and Tracy both maintain a constant speed.]

4 (a) From $t = 2$ to $t = 5$, speed increases uniformly from 2 to $8\,\mathrm{m\,s}^{-1}$.

Using areas,

when $t = 3$, $\dfrac{ds}{dt} = 4$ and $s = 4 + \frac{1}{2}(2 + 4) = 7$;

when $t = 4$, $\dfrac{ds}{dt} = 6$ and $s = 7 + \frac{1}{2}(4 + 6) = 12$;

when $t = 5$, $\dfrac{ds}{dt} = 8$ and $s = 12 + \frac{1}{2}(6 + 8) = 19$.

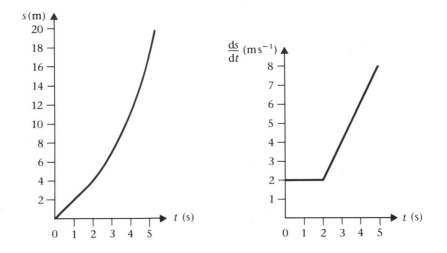

(b) The distance covered is 19 metres.

5 (a) A moves at constant speed.

(b) B moves with a constant rate of increase of speed, up to twice the speed of A.

(c) After 2 seconds   (d) After 4 seconds

2.6 Investigating speed

> The Highway Code states:
>
> On an open road, in good conditions, a two-second gap between cars should be sufficient.
>
> What is meant by a two-second gap?

This means that if there is a gap of 50 metres, say, between the front of your car and the rear of the car in front, it should take you at least two seconds to cover that distance. This means that you should not be travelling at more than $25\,\mathrm{m\,s}^{-1}$.

3 Vectors

3.1 Introduction

Write down some examples of scalar quantities.

Can you think of any vector quantities other than displacement?

Some scalar quantities are time, speed, area and volume. Another is mass, which will be discussed in chapter 5.

Other vector quantities are velocity (discussed in chapter 4), momentum (discussed in chapter 5) and force (discussed in chapter 6).

E X E R C I S E   1

(Answers are given to 1 decimal place where necessary.)

1 (a)

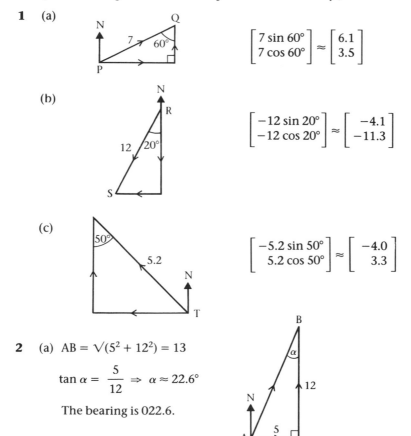

$$\begin{bmatrix} 7 \sin 60° \\ 7 \cos 60° \end{bmatrix} \approx \begin{bmatrix} 6.1 \\ 3.5 \end{bmatrix}$$

(b)

$$\begin{bmatrix} -12 \sin 20° \\ -12 \cos 20° \end{bmatrix} \approx \begin{bmatrix} -4.1 \\ -11.3 \end{bmatrix}$$

(c)

$$\begin{bmatrix} -5.2 \sin 50° \\ 5.2 \cos 50° \end{bmatrix} \approx \begin{bmatrix} -4.0 \\ 3.3 \end{bmatrix}$$

2 (a) $AB = \sqrt{(5^2 + 12^2)} = 13$

$\tan \alpha = \dfrac{5}{12} \Rightarrow \alpha \approx 22.6°$

The bearing is 022.6.

(b)

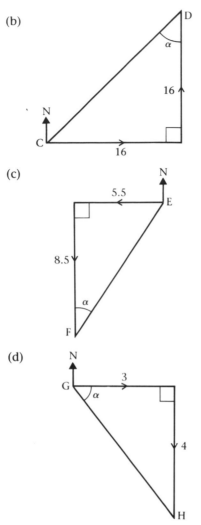

$CD = \sqrt{(16^2 + 16^2)} \approx 22.6$

$\alpha = 45°$

The bearing is 045°.

(c)

$EF = \sqrt{(5.5^2 + 8.5^2)} \approx 10.1$

$\tan \alpha = \dfrac{5.5}{8.5} \Rightarrow \alpha \approx 32.9°$

The bearing is $(180 + 32.9)° = 212.9°$.

(d)

$GH = \sqrt{(3^2 + 4^2)} = 5$

$\tan \alpha = \dfrac{4}{3} \Rightarrow \alpha \approx 53.1°$

The bearing is $(90 + 53.1)° = 143.1°$

3.2 Vectors and maps

Confirm your understanding of six-figure map references by:

(a) writing down the references of Phoebe's Point and Cadythew Rock;

(b) stating what can be found at 002480 and at 038483;

(c) changing 024473 and 032505 into distance coordinates.

(a) 033499,   016408 (taken at the middle)

(b) Dairy,   The Bite

(c) $\begin{bmatrix} 2.4 \\ 47.3 \end{bmatrix}$, $\begin{bmatrix} 3.2 \\ 50.5 \end{bmatrix}$

EXERCISE 2

(a) Distance from C to B = $\sqrt{(12.7^2 + 20.1^2)} \approx 23.8\,\text{km}$

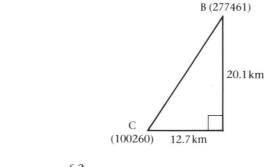

(b) $\tan \alpha = \dfrac{6.3}{29.7} \Rightarrow \alpha \approx 12.0°$

The bearing of D from A is about 102°.

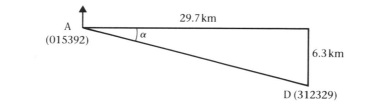

(c) $\overrightarrow{BD} = \begin{bmatrix} 31.2 - 22.7 \\ 32.9 - 46.1 \end{bmatrix} = \begin{bmatrix} 8.5 \\ -13.2 \end{bmatrix}$

$BD = \sqrt{(8.5^2 + 13.2^2)} = 15.7\,\text{km}$

$\tan \alpha = \dfrac{13.2}{8.5} \Rightarrow \alpha \approx 57.2°$

The bearing is $90° + 57.2° = 147.2°$.

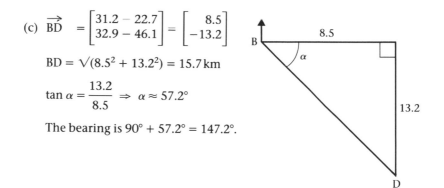

(d) The bearing of $\overrightarrow{DB}$ is $147.2° + 180° = 327.2°$.

(e) $\overrightarrow{AB} = \begin{bmatrix} 22.7 - 1.5 \\ 46.1 - 39.2 \end{bmatrix} = \begin{bmatrix} 21.2 \\ 6.9 \end{bmatrix}$

$\overrightarrow{CD} = \begin{bmatrix} 31.2 - 10 \\ 32.9 - 26 \end{bmatrix} = \begin{bmatrix} 21.2 \\ 6.9 \end{bmatrix}$

Hence $\overrightarrow{AB} = \overrightarrow{CD} \Rightarrow AB = CD$, and AB is in the same direction as CD.

3.3 Adding vectors

EXERCISE 3

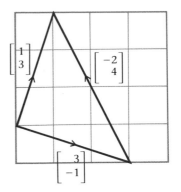

1 $\begin{bmatrix} 3 \\ -1 \end{bmatrix} + \begin{bmatrix} -2 \\ 4 \end{bmatrix} = \begin{bmatrix} 1 \\ 3 \end{bmatrix}$

2 (a) **u** + **v**　(b) **u** + 2**v**　(c) **v** − **u**

3 $\begin{bmatrix} -2 \\ -3 \end{bmatrix} + \begin{bmatrix} 5 \\ -7 \end{bmatrix} + \begin{bmatrix} 16 \\ 4 \end{bmatrix} = \begin{bmatrix} 19 \\ -6 \end{bmatrix}$

Missing vector = $\begin{bmatrix} -9 \\ 4 \end{bmatrix}$

4 (a) D (115350)

(b) $\overrightarrow{AD} = \begin{bmatrix} 11.5 - 2.5 \\ 35 - 10.5 \end{bmatrix} = \begin{bmatrix} 9 \\ 24.5 \end{bmatrix}$

$\overrightarrow{BC} = \begin{bmatrix} 19.5 - 10.5 \\ 40 - 15.5 \end{bmatrix} = \begin{bmatrix} 9 \\ 24.5 \end{bmatrix}$

$\overrightarrow{AD} = \overrightarrow{BC}$

(c) AD = BC and AD ∥ BC ⇒ ABCD is a parallelogram

3.4 Using vectors

Find the displacement vector $\overrightarrow{SF}$ and hence the distance and bearing the single boat must sail to rejoin the fleet.

From the vector triangle $\overrightarrow{PS} + \overrightarrow{SF} = \overrightarrow{PF}$,

$\overrightarrow{SF} = \overrightarrow{PF} - \overrightarrow{PS} = \begin{bmatrix} 8.66 \\ -5.00 \end{bmatrix} - \begin{bmatrix} 2.83 \\ 2.83 \end{bmatrix} = \begin{bmatrix} 5.83 \\ -7.83 \end{bmatrix}$

The column vector is now converted back to a distance and bearing.

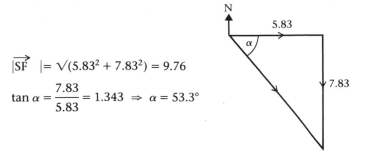

$|\overrightarrow{SF}| = \sqrt{(5.83^2 + 7.83^2)} = 9.76$

$\tan \alpha = \dfrac{7.83}{5.83} = 1.343 \Rightarrow \alpha = 53.3°$

Thus, to rejoin the fleet the single boat sails on a bearing of 143.3° for a distance of 9.76 km.

E X E R C I S E   4

1 $\overrightarrow{PQ} = \begin{bmatrix} -100 \cos 45° \\ 100 \sin 45° \end{bmatrix} \approx \begin{bmatrix} -70.7 \\ 70.7 \end{bmatrix}$

$\overrightarrow{AQ} = \begin{bmatrix} 83 - 70.7 \\ 70.7 \end{bmatrix} = \begin{bmatrix} 12.3 \\ 70.7 \end{bmatrix}$

$\overrightarrow{AQ} = \sqrt{(12.3^2 + 70.7^2)} \approx 71.8$

Airport Q is closer to the aircraft by 11.2 km

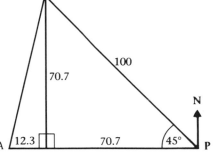

2 $\overrightarrow{PS} = \begin{bmatrix} 20 \cos 37° \\ -20 \sin 37° \end{bmatrix} = \begin{bmatrix} 15.97 \\ -12.04 \end{bmatrix}$

$\overrightarrow{HS} \approx \begin{bmatrix} 15.97 - 5 \\ -12.04 \end{bmatrix} \approx \begin{bmatrix} 10.97 \\ -12.04 \end{bmatrix}$

$\overrightarrow{HS} \approx \sqrt{(10.97^2 + 12.04^2)} \approx 16.3$

$\tan \theta \approx \dfrac{12.04}{10.97} \Rightarrow \theta \approx 47.7°$

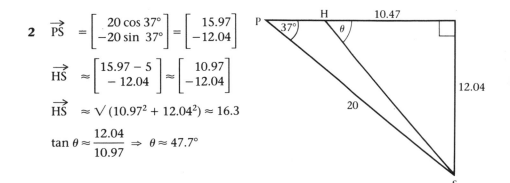

The helicopter has to fly in the direction 137.7° for a distance of 16.3 km.

3 The displacement westwards of the boat is 9 sin 38° km each hour, and the time taken for its displacement westwards to be 4.7 km is

$$\frac{4.7}{9 \sin 38°} \approx 0.85 \text{ hour} = 51 \text{ minutes}$$

Hence it will be due north of Black Cap Light at 3:06 a.m.

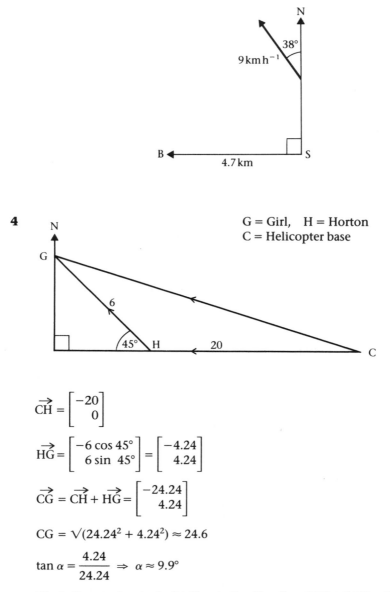

4   G = Girl, H = Horton
C = Helicopter base

$$\overrightarrow{CH} = \begin{bmatrix} -20 \\ 0 \end{bmatrix}$$

$$\overrightarrow{HG} = \begin{bmatrix} -6 \cos 45° \\ 6 \sin 45° \end{bmatrix} = \begin{bmatrix} -4.24 \\ 4.24 \end{bmatrix}$$

$$\overrightarrow{CG} = \overrightarrow{CH} + \overrightarrow{HG} = \begin{bmatrix} -24.24 \\ 4.24 \end{bmatrix}$$

$$CG = \sqrt{(24.24^2 + 4.24^2)} \approx 24.6$$

$$\tan \alpha = \frac{4.24}{24.24} \Rightarrow \alpha \approx 9.9°$$

The helicopter has to fly 24.6 km in the direction $(270 + 9.9)° = 279.9°$.

5   The displacement of HMS *Battledore* from port at 15:00 is

$$\frac{2}{5}\begin{bmatrix} 15\sin 61° \\ -15\cos 61° \end{bmatrix} + \frac{7}{20}\begin{bmatrix} -15\sin 17° \\ 15\cos 17° \end{bmatrix} = \begin{bmatrix} 6\sin 61° - 5.25\sin 17° \\ -6\cos 61° + 5.25\cos 17° \end{bmatrix}$$

The displacement of HMS *Shuttlecock* from port at 15:00 is

$$\frac{1}{2}\begin{bmatrix} -12\sin 25° \\ -12\cos 25° \end{bmatrix} = \begin{bmatrix} -6\sin 25° \\ -6\cos 25° \end{bmatrix}$$

The displacement of HMS *Shuttlecock* from HMS *Battledore* is

$$\begin{bmatrix} -6\sin 25° - 6\sin 61° + 5.25\sin 17° \\ -6\cos 25° + 6\cos 61° - 5.25\cos 17° \end{bmatrix} \approx \begin{bmatrix} -6.2485 \\ -7.5496 \end{bmatrix}$$

$d \approx \sqrt{(6.2485^2 + 7.5496^2)} \approx 9.80.$

So at 15:00 the ships are about 9.80 nautical miles apart.

Time taken to meet $\approx \dfrac{9.80}{20} = 0.49$ hour $= 29\frac{1}{2}$ min

$\tan\phi = \dfrac{6.2495}{7.5496} \Rightarrow \phi \approx 39.6°$

HMS *Battledore* proceeds on bearing 219.6°.

3.5   Position and displacement

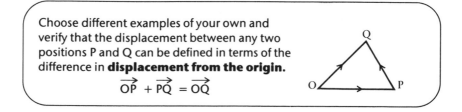

Choose different examples of your own and verify that the displacement between any two positions P and Q can be defined in terms of the difference in **displacement from the origin**.

$$\overrightarrow{OP} + \overrightarrow{PQ} = \overrightarrow{OQ}$$

This result is obvious in view of the fact that going from O to Q is simply the resultant of going from O to P to Q, i.e. $\overrightarrow{OQ} = \overrightarrow{OP} + \overrightarrow{PQ}$.

EXERCISE 5

1

	(a)	(b)	(c)	(d)
Original position vector	$\begin{bmatrix} 200 \\ 90 \end{bmatrix}$	$\begin{bmatrix} 7 \\ -7 \end{bmatrix}$	$\begin{bmatrix} -32 \\ 16 \end{bmatrix}$	$\begin{bmatrix} -88 \\ -262 \end{bmatrix}$
New position vector	$\begin{bmatrix} 326 \\ 81 \end{bmatrix}$	$\begin{bmatrix} 73 \\ -81 \end{bmatrix}$	$\begin{bmatrix} -15 \\ -4 \end{bmatrix}$	$\begin{bmatrix} -10 \\ -8 \end{bmatrix}$
Displacement	$\begin{bmatrix} 126 \\ -9 \end{bmatrix}$	$\begin{bmatrix} 66 \\ -74 \end{bmatrix}$	$\begin{bmatrix} 17 \\ -20 \end{bmatrix}$	$\begin{bmatrix} 78 \\ 254 \end{bmatrix}$

2 (a) The new position vector is $\begin{bmatrix} 5.7 \\ 2.6 \end{bmatrix} + \begin{bmatrix} 0.9 \\ 0.2 \end{bmatrix} + \begin{bmatrix} 1.4 \\ -0.7 \end{bmatrix} + \begin{bmatrix} 1.2 \\ 0.5 \end{bmatrix} = \begin{bmatrix} 9.2 \\ 2.6 \end{bmatrix}$

(b) The total displacement is $\begin{bmatrix} 3.5 \\ 0 \end{bmatrix}$

(c) The boat has travelled

$\sqrt{(0.9^2 + 0.2^2)} + \sqrt{(1.4^2 + 0.7^2)} + \sqrt{(1.2^2 + 0.5^2)}$
$= 0.922 + 1.565 + 1.3$
$= 3.79\,\text{km}$, to 3 significant figures

4 Velocity

4.2 Average speed and average velocity

EXERCISE 1

1 Time for outward journey $= \dfrac{20}{40} = 0.5$ hour

Time for return journey $= \dfrac{20}{80} = 0.25$ hour

Time for total journey $= 0.75$ hour

Total distance covered $= 40\,\text{km}$

Average speed $= \dfrac{40}{0.75}\,\text{km}\,\text{h}^{-1} \approx 53.3\,\text{km}\,\text{h}^{-1}$

2   Time taken over first stage = 1 hour

Time taken to travel d km of second stage = $\dfrac{d}{60}$ hours

Total length of journey = $(30 + d)$ km

Total time of journey = $\left(1 + \dfrac{d}{60}\right)$ hour

Hence

$$45\left(1 + \dfrac{d}{60}\right) = 30 + d$$

$$\Rightarrow 45 + \dfrac{3d}{4} = 30 + d$$

$$\Rightarrow \dfrac{d}{4} = 15$$

$$\Rightarrow d = 60$$

Length of second stage = 60 km

3   Time taken to go from A to B = 30 + 20 + 10 = 60 seconds

Total distance = 120 m

Average speed = $\dfrac{120}{60}$ m s^{-1} = 2 m s^{-1}

Total displacement = 60 m due north

Average velocity = 1 m s^{-1} due north

4   An object travelling at constant speed, for example a car moving round a curve, will change its direction of motion continuously and hence cannot have constant velocity. However, a train travelling along a straight portion of track with constant speed will have constant velocity since its direction of motion is unaltered.

An aircraft flying with constant velocity must be moving with constant speed in a fixed direction.

To sum up, an object travelling with constant speed is not travelling with constant velocity, unless the motion takes place in a straight line. On the other hand, a constant velocity means motion in a straight line in a given direction with constant speed; hence, constant velocity implies constant speed.

5   If the average velocity is 50 km h^{-1} due east, the end of the journey, B, must be due east of the start A. Unless the car travels due east throughout the journey (when the average speed would be 50 km h^{-1}), the distance travelled must be greater than the length of the straight line AB. Hence the average speed must be greater than 50 km h^{-1}.

6 (a) Taking $\pi = \frac{22}{7}$, the distance covered by the particle around the semi-circular path is $\frac{22}{7} \times 7\,\text{m} = 22\,\text{m}$. If the speed increases uniformly with time, the average speed is

$$\frac{8 + 14}{2}\,\text{m}\,\text{s}^{-1} = 11\,\text{m}\,\text{s}^{-1}$$

Hence the time taken to complete the path is $\frac{22}{11} = 2$ seconds.

(b) The speed is increasing each second by $3\,\text{m}\,\text{s}^{-1}$. Hence it takes 1 second to reach $11\,\text{m}\,\text{s}^{-2}$.

If the distance covered in that one second is d m, the average speed is $d\,\text{m}\,\text{s}^{-1}$. So

$$d = \frac{8 + 11}{2} = 9\tfrac{1}{2}$$

The particle's speed is $11\,\text{m}\,\text{s}^{-1}$ when the particle has travelled $9\tfrac{1}{2}\,\text{m}$ along the path.

(c) The displacement in travelling from A to B is $14\,\text{m}$ in the direction of $\overrightarrow{AB}$ and this takes 2 seconds. Hence, the average velocity is $7\,\text{m}\,\text{s}^{-1}$ in the direction of $\overrightarrow{AB}$.

7E As the length of the track is not given in the question you should choose a suitable numerical value; $40\,\text{km}$ is recommended. The graphical solutions are easiest.

(a)

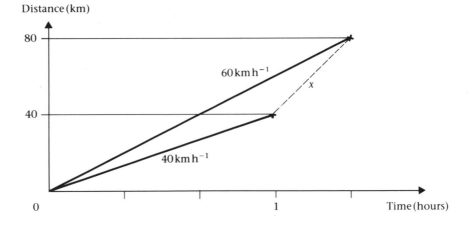

This shows that it must travel $40\,\text{km}$ in 20 minutes.
The speed required is thus $120\,\text{km}\,\text{h}^{-1}$

(b) Distance (km)

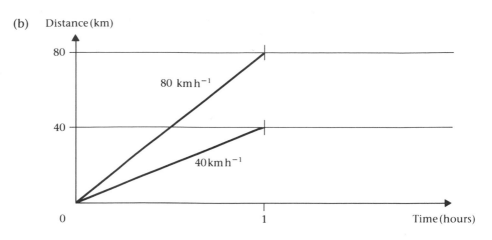

Clearly it is impossible to travel 40 km in no time at all. Therefore an average speed of $80\,\text{km}\,\text{h}^{-1}$ or greater is impossible to achieve.

4.3   Straight line motion

EXERCISE 2

1 (a) From the (t, x) graph, after 9 seconds, the displacement = 0.

From the $\left(t, \dfrac{dx}{dt}\right)$ graph for the first T seconds, displacement = $4T$ metres and for the next $(9 - T)$ seconds, displacement = $-2(9 - T)$ metres.

The total displacement is $4T - 2(9 - T) = 6T - 18 = 0 \Rightarrow T = 3$.

   (b) When $t = 3$, $x = 12$; so the distance travelled after 9 seconds is $2 \times 12 = 24$ metres.

   (c) The displacement after 9 seconds is 0 metres.

2 (a) For the motion, $x = 6t - 5t^2 \Rightarrow \dfrac{dx}{dt} = 6 - 10t$

When $t = 0.25$, $\dfrac{dx}{dt} = 3.5$

When $t = 3.5$, $\dfrac{dx}{dt} = -34$

The velocity of the ball after 0.25 seconds is $3.5\,\text{m}\,\text{s}^{-1}$ vertically upwards, and after 4 seconds is $34\,\text{m}\,\text{s}^{-1}$ vertically downwards.

Alternatively the (t, x) graph could be drawn and the gradient measurer used to find $\dfrac{dx}{dt}$ (the answers then would only be approximate).

   (b) The displacement after the first 5 seconds is $(30 - 125) = -95$ metres.

Average velocity $= \dfrac{-95}{5} = -19\,\text{m}\,\text{s}^{-1}$

113

3 (a)

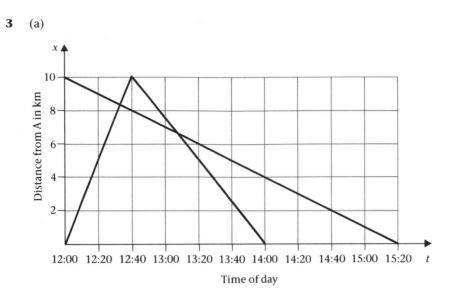

Time of day

(b) Pass at $t_1 = 12{:}33$, distance from A $\approx 8.3\,\text{km}$

Pass at $t_2 = 13{:}07$, distance from A $\approx 6.7\,\text{km}$

(c) From t_1 to 12:40, the distance apart increases. From 12:40 to t_2, the distance apart decreases. The time when they are the greatest distance apart is 12:40.

4 (a) By the use of the gradient measurer it can be established that $\dfrac{dy}{dt} = -10t$ from $t = 0$ to $t = 1.4$.

Between $t = 1.4$ and $t = 3.6$, the graph is symmetrical about $t = 2.5$.

By the use of the gradient measurer it can be established when $t = 1.4$ that $\dfrac{dy}{dt} = 11$ and the graph of $\left(t, \dfrac{dy}{dt}\right)$ is a straight line of gradient -10.

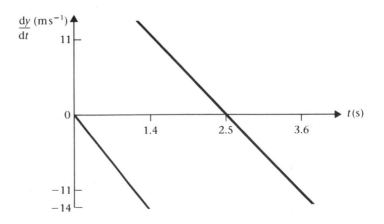

(b) At $t = 1.4$ seconds, the ball hits the ground with a speed of $14\,\mathrm{ms^{-1}}$ (velocity $-14\,\mathrm{ms^{-1}}$) and rebounds with a speed of $11\,\mathrm{ms^{-1}}$ (velocity $11\,\mathrm{ms^{-1}}$)

(c)

(d) When $t = 1$, ball's speed $= 10\,\mathrm{ms^{-1}}$

4.4 Change in velocity

EXERCISE 3

1 (a) $13\,\mathrm{ms^{-1}}$ due west (b) $13\,\mathrm{ms^{-1}}$ due east

(c)

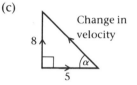

Change in velocity

$\sqrt{(8^2 + 5^2)} = 9.43$ (3 s.f.)

$\tan \alpha = \frac{8}{5} \Rightarrow \alpha = 58.0°$

2

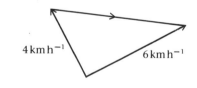

4 km h^{-1} 6 km h^{-1}

The change in velocity is $7.2\,\mathrm{km\,h^{-1}}$ in direction 079°.

3 Resultant velocity of aeroplane $= \begin{bmatrix} 200 \\ 10 \end{bmatrix} + \begin{bmatrix} -30 \\ 40 \end{bmatrix}\mathrm{km\,h^{-1}} = \begin{bmatrix} 170 \\ 50 \end{bmatrix}\mathrm{km\,h^{-1}}$

Magnitude of velocity $= \sqrt{(170^2 + 50^2)}\,\mathrm{km\,h^{-1}} \approx 177.2\,\mathrm{km\,h^{-1}}$

$$\tan \theta = \frac{170}{50} \Rightarrow \theta \approx 73.6°$$

The resultant velocity of the aeroplane is $177.2\,\mathrm{km\,h^{-1}}$ in direction 073.6°.

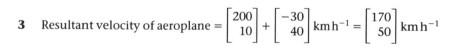

N   50 km h^{-1} θ 170 km h^{-1}

115

4 Change in velocity $= \begin{bmatrix} 6 \\ 6 \end{bmatrix} \mathrm{m\,s^{-1}}$

Its magnitude is $\sqrt{(6^2 + 6^2)}\,\mathrm{m\,s^{-1}} \approx 8.5\,\mathrm{m\,s^{-1}}$. Its direction is 045°.

5 Velocity of the wind $\approx 14.0\,\mathrm{km\,h^{-1}}$ in direction 142°.

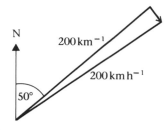

4.5 Resultant velocity

> Now try to generalise your problem for different velocities of the river.

Set up a model

Let the velocity of the river be $U\,\mathrm{m\,s^{-1}}$ and suppose that you wish to row directly across the river.

Analyse the problem

The resultant velocity, V, is $\sqrt{(2^2 - U^2)}$.

The direction in which you must row makes angle α with the bank, where $\cos \alpha = \frac{1}{2}U$. This gives a graph.

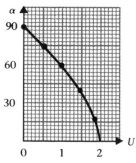

U	0	$\frac{1}{2}$	1	$1\frac{1}{2}$	2	1.9
α	90	75.5	60	41.4	0	18.2

Interpret /validate

Since $V = \sqrt{(2^2 - U^2)}$, U must be less than 2 for you to be able to cross the river. ($2^2 - U^2$ must be positive for real V.) As U increases, V decreases and it takes longer to cross the river.

The graph shows that as U increases the angle at which you must row decreases. You must aim further and further upstream.

EXERCISE 4

1

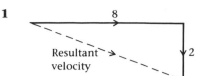

By Pythagoras, her speed is

$$\sqrt{(8^2 + 2^2)} = 8.25\,\text{m}\,\text{s}^{-1} \text{ (3 s.f.)}$$

2 $\cos\theta \approx \dfrac{1}{1.5} \Rightarrow \theta \approx 48°$

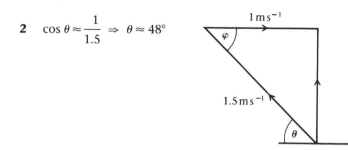

The girl should point her canoe upriver making an angle of 48° with the bank.

Resultant speed $= \sqrt{(1.5^2 - 1^2)}\,\text{ms}^{-1}$

Time taken to cross river $= \dfrac{100}{\text{Resultant speed}} \approx 89\,\text{seconds}.$

Assumptions made:

- she can paddle immediately with speed $1.5\,\text{m}\,\text{s}^{-1}$;
- she can maintain both this speed and the direction throughout the motion;
- the speed of the river is the same throughout its width.

3   By scale drawing:

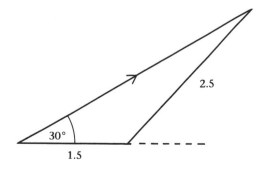

He should swim at an angle of 48° to the bank. The resultant speed will be $3.7\,\text{km}\,\text{h}^{-1}$.

4

Sketch

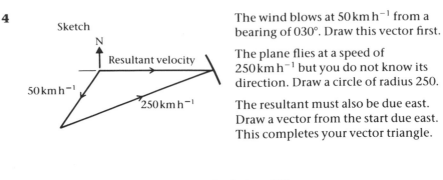

The wind blows at $50\,km\,h^{-1}$ from a bearing of $030°$. Draw this vector first.

The plane flies at a speed of $250\,km\,h^{-1}$ but you do not know its direction. Draw a circle of radius 250.

The resultant must also be due east. Draw a vector from the start due east. This completes your vector triangle.

Scale drawing   **Scale** $1\,cm:25\,km$

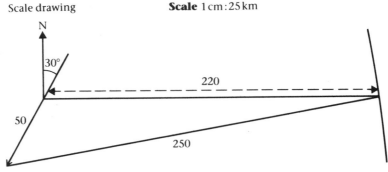

By measurement, the resultant velocity is about $220\,km\,h^{-1}$ due east. The plane must head on a bearing of $080°$.

The plane must cover $100\,km$ so the time taken is $\dfrac{100}{220} = 0.4545$ hour.

This is approximately 27 minutes.

5 Changes in motion

5.1 The 'quantity of motion'

What do you understand by the word 'mass'?

How can you compare the masses of different objects? Is it helpful to think in terms of the size or volume of the objects? Can you use the weights of objects to compare their masses?

We often tend to judge the mass of an object, on sight, by its size. We can be surprised if it is small but very dense (e.g. made of lead) or large but of low density (e.g. polystyrene foam).

The relationship between mass and volume, usually expressed as

$$\text{Density} = \frac{\text{Mass}}{\text{Volume}} \quad \text{or} \quad \text{Mass} = \text{Volume} \times \text{Density}$$

allows us to compare the masses of objects of the same average density simply by measuring their volumes (e.g. by the amount of water they displace).

The Earth pulls an object towards its centre with a force proportional to the object's mass. This means we can compare masses of objects by comparing their weights.

5.3 Momentum

EXERCISE 1

1 (b) and (c) have the same momentum, which is $15\,\text{kg}\,\text{m}\,\text{s}^{-1}$ eastwards. (a) is in a different direction.

2 $70 \times \begin{bmatrix} 3 \\ 4 \end{bmatrix} = \begin{bmatrix} 210 \\ 280 \end{bmatrix} \text{kg}\,\text{m}\,\text{s}^{-1}$ which has magnitude

$70 \times \sqrt{(3^2 + 4^2)} = 70 \times 5 = 350\,\text{kg}\,\text{m}\,\text{s}^{-1}$ in the direction making angle $\tan^{-1}\frac{3}{4}$ with north, i.e. bearing 037°.

3 (a)

The car has three times the speed of the truck but only one tenth of its mass.

(b)

The speedboat has a greater speed than the ferry but a much smaller mass.

(c)

The jeep is slightly faster than the rhino but the rhino is slightly heavier.

(d)   Bullet ———————→———————

       Cricket ball ————→———

Estimates for the masses and speeds are:

bullet: mass 20 grams, speed $500 \, \mathrm{m\,s^{-1}}$;

cricket ball: mass 156 grams, speed $40 \, \mathrm{m\,s^{-1}}$.

5.4   Conservation of momentum

> What assumptions have been made in answering this question? Are they reasonable?

The law of conservation of momentum has been assumed.

It has also been assumed that **all** of the 140 kg moves with the same velocity just after the collision. This is **not** a reasonable assumption as the motions of Louise and Eddie will differ initially from those of their toboggans. However, if they remain on their toboggans and if friction has no appreciable effect, then the motion will soon settle down into one of a uniform speed of approximately $0.15 \, \mathrm{m\,s^{-1}}$.

EXERCISE 2

1 (a)   Momentum before   Momentum after

       ————20————→   ←————10v————

$20 = 10v \;\Rightarrow\; v = 2$

The velocity of B has magnitude $2 \, \mathrm{m\,s^{-1}}$.

(b)   Momentum before   Momentum after

       ——15——→ ←——20——   ←——10—— ——10v——→

$15 - 20 = 10v - 10 \;\Rightarrow\; v = \frac{1}{2}$

The velocity of B has magnitude $\frac{1}{2} \, \mathrm{m\,s^{-1}}$.

(c)

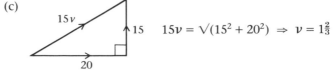

$15v = \sqrt{(15^2 + 20^2)} \;\Rightarrow\; v = 1\frac{2}{3}$

This is a velocity of $1\frac{2}{3} \, \mathrm{m\,s^{-1}}$ at an angle of $\tan^{-1} \frac{3}{4}$ to the original direction of the motion of A.

2 If $v \, \mathrm{ms}^{-1}$ was the speed of the car just before impact, by conservation of momentum:

$$1200v + 2000 \times 0 = (1200 + 2000) \times 7 \implies v \approx 19 \, \mathrm{ms}^{-1}$$

3 $3 \, \mathrm{ms}^{-1}$

4 Let the mass of Q be m kg. Taking the initial velocity of P as positive and any velocity in the opposite direction as negative, by conservation of momentum:

$$2 \times 5 + m \times (-4) = 2 \times (-1) + m \times 2$$

Hence $m = 2$.

5

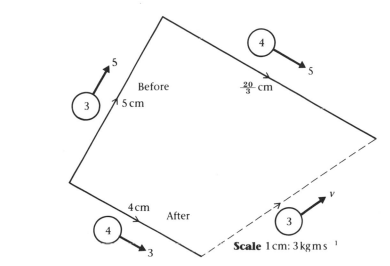

The final velocity of the 3 kg mass is $\frac{17}{3} \approx 5.7 \, \mathrm{ms}^{-1}$ on bearing 058°.

5.5 Change in momentum

EXERCISE 3

1 The speed increases from $18.0\dot{5} \, \mathrm{ms}^{-1}$ to $33.\dot{3} \, \mathrm{ms}^{-1}$. The initial momentum is $180\,556 \, \mathrm{kg \, ms}^{-1}$ and the final momentum is $333\,333 \, \mathrm{kg \, ms}^{-1}$.

The change in momentum is $152\,777 \, \mathrm{kg \, ms}^{-1}$
$= 153\,000 \, \mathrm{kg \, ms}^{-1}$ to 3 significant figures

2 (a) Initial momentum $= 30\,000 \, \mathrm{kg \, ms}^{-1}$
New momentum $= 15\,000 \, \mathrm{kg \, ms}^{-1}$

The new speed is $7.5 \, \mathrm{ms}^{-1}$.

(b) Initial momentum $= 150\,000 \, \mathrm{kg \, ms}^{-1}$
New momentum $= 135\,000 \, \mathrm{kg \, ms}^{-1}$

The new speed is $13.5 \, \mathrm{ms}^{-1}$.

3

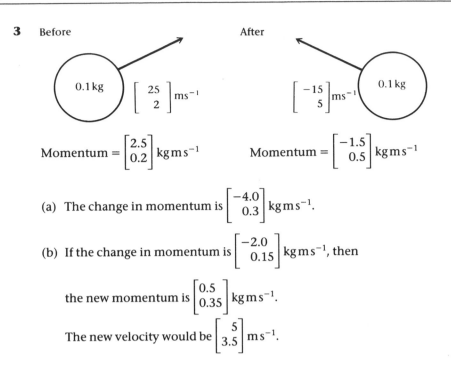

Before   After

0.1 kg $\begin{bmatrix} 25 \\ 2 \end{bmatrix}$ ms^{-1} $\begin{bmatrix} -15 \\ 5 \end{bmatrix}$ ms^{-1} 0.1 kg

Momentum $= \begin{bmatrix} 2.5 \\ 0.2 \end{bmatrix}$ kg m s^{-1} Momentum $= \begin{bmatrix} -1.5 \\ 0.5 \end{bmatrix}$ kg m s^{-1}

(a) The change in momentum is $\begin{bmatrix} -4.0 \\ 0.3 \end{bmatrix}$ kg m s^{-1}.

(b) If the change in momentum is $\begin{bmatrix} -2.0 \\ 0.15 \end{bmatrix}$ kg m s^{-1}, then

the new momentum is $\begin{bmatrix} 0.5 \\ 0.35 \end{bmatrix}$ kg m s^{-1}.

The new velocity would be $\begin{bmatrix} 5 \\ 3.5 \end{bmatrix}$ m s^{-1}.

6 Force

6.2 Newton's second law of motion

> One form of Newton's second law, for a constant resultant force, is
>
> Change of momentum = Resultant force × Time
>
> Explain how this form is equivalent to the one given above.

The resultant force is equal to the change of momentum each second. So, if the resultant force is constant, the total change of momentum will be simply the product of the resultant force with the time elapsed.

EXERCISE 1

1

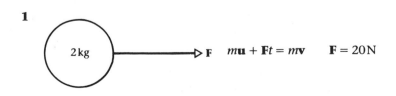

2 kg   →F $m\mathbf{u} + \mathbf{F}t = m\mathbf{v}$ F = 20N

$t = 0, \quad u = 0$ $2 \times 0 + 20 \times 1 = 2v$
$t = 1, \quad v = ?$ $\Rightarrow v = 10\,\mathrm{m\,s}^{-1}$

$t = 1, \quad u = 10$ $2 \times 10 + 20 \times 1 = 2v$
$t = 2, \quad v = ?$ $\Rightarrow v = 20\,\mathrm{m\,s}^{-1}$

$t = 2, \quad u = 20$ $2 \times 20 + 20 \times 1 = 2v$
$t = 3, \quad v = ?$ $\Rightarrow v = 30\,\mathrm{m\,s}^{-1}$

$t = 3, \quad u = 30$ $2 \times 30 + 20 \times 1 = 2v$
$t = 4, \quad v = ?$ $\Rightarrow v = 40\,\mathrm{m\,s}^{-1}$

The speed is being increased by a constant amount each second.

2    $m\mathbf{u} + \mathbf{F}t = m\mathbf{v}$ $t = 5, m = 0.2,$ take north as positive.

$$0.2 \times (-1.5) + F \times 5 = 0.2 \times 2$$
$$\Rightarrow F = 0.14$$

A force of $0.14\,\mathrm{N}$ is needed, acting due north.

3    $m\mathbf{u} + \mathbf{F}t = m\mathbf{v}$ $m = 900$ $F = -1250\,\mathrm{N}$

$$v = \frac{48 \times 1000}{60 \times 60} = \frac{40}{3}\,\mathrm{m\,s}^{-1} \qquad u = \frac{72 \times 1000}{60 \times 60} = 20\,\mathrm{m\,s}^{-1}$$

$$900 \times 20 - 1250 \times t = \frac{900 \times 40}{3} \quad \Rightarrow t = 4.8$$

The time taken is 4.8 seconds.

4   The momentum of the train is $35\,000 \times 0.3\,\mathrm{kg\,m\,s}^{-1}$.

$$2F = 10\,500 \ \Rightarrow \ F = 5250$$

A force of $5250\,\mathrm{N}$ is required.

5   The change in momentum is $150 \times 3 = 450\,\mathrm{kg\,m\,s}^{-1}$.

$$200v = 450 \ \Rightarrow \ v = 2.25$$

The speed is $2.25\,\mathrm{m\,s}^{-1}$.

6.3   Newton's third law of motion

EXERCISE 2

1   The weight of the apple is the gravitational force due to the attraction of the Earth. Thus the 'other body' is the Earth. The total momentum of the Earth and the apple is conserved. This implies that the Earth moves towards the apple as well as the apple moving towards the Earth. This does, in fact, happen but the mass of the Earth is so much greater than that of the apple that the effect is far too small to measure.

2

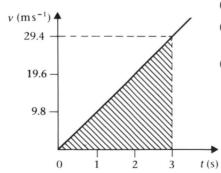

There is a gravitational force exerted by the Sun on the Earth and a force, equal in magnitude and opposite in direction, exerted by the Earth on the Sun. Once again, the total momentum of the system is conserved. However, the mass of the Sun is far greater than that of the Earth and so the effect on the Earth's velocity is much greater that the effect on the velocity of the Sun.

The pull of the Sun causes a change in the Earth's velocity but not its speed. This motion must, of course, satisfy Newton's second law.

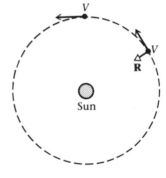

6.4   Weight and change of momentum

EXERCISE 3

1

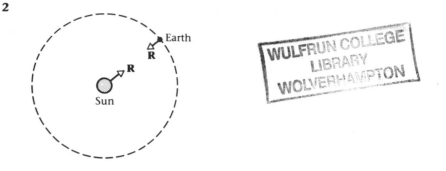

(a) When $t = 3$, $v = 29.4\,\mathrm{m\,s^{-1}}$.

(b) The distance fallen is the area under the graph, 44.1 metres.

(c) When $t = 3.5$, $v = 9.8 \times 3.5$.
$s = vt = 60$ metres.
The cliff is 60 metres high.

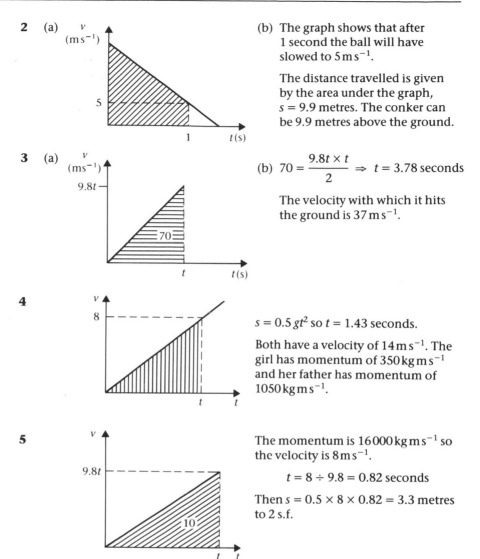

2 (a)

(b) The graph shows that after 1 second the ball will have slowed to $5\,\mathrm{m\,s^{-1}}$.

The distance travelled is given by the area under the graph, $s = 9.9$ metres. The conker can be 9.9 metres above the ground.

3 (a)

(b) $70 = \dfrac{9.8t \times t}{2} \Rightarrow t = 3.78$ seconds

The velocity with which it hits the ground is $37\,\mathrm{m\,s^{-1}}$.

4

$s = 0.5\,gt^2$ so $t = 1.43$ seconds.

Both have a velocity of $14\,\mathrm{m\,s^{-1}}$. The girl has momentum of $350\,\mathrm{kg\,m\,s^{-1}}$ and her father has momentum of $1050\,\mathrm{kg\,m\,s^{-1}}$.

5

The momentum is $16000\,\mathrm{kg\,m\,s^{-1}}$ so the velocity is $8\,\mathrm{m\,s^{-1}}$.

$t = 8 \div 9.8 = 0.82$ seconds

Then $s = 0.5 \times 8 \times 0.82 = 3.3$ metres to 2 s.f.